Horace

Greek and Latin Studies
Classical Literature and its Influence

Editors

C. D. N. Costa and J. W. Binns

Greek and Latin Studies
Classical Literature and its Influence

Horace

Edited by
C. D. N. COSTA

Routledge & Kegan Paul: LONDON AND BOSTON

First published in 1973
by Routledge & Kegan Paul Ltd
Broadway House, 68–74 Carter Lane,
London EC4V 5EL and
9 Park Street
Boston, Mass. 02108, U.S.A.
Printed in Great Britain by
The Camelot Press Ltd, London and Southampton

ISBN 0 7100 7597 9

Library of Congress Catalog Card
Number 73-77038

Contents

To the memory
of
D. R. Dudley

Introduction

It is fashionable to be defensive about the appearance of another book on a popular writer: with a poet as many-sided as Horace this is unnecessary. Though there has scarcely been a time when he was out of favour it is hard to imagine that critics could run out of original things to say about him – which is not to deny that he has had his share of nonsensical criticism and survived undimmed. We owe it to the greatest authors to try always to look at them with fresh eyes, and a sign of the Horatian times is that a massive commentary on the *Odes* is currently being written in Oxford.

On this assumption, that we cannot have too many serious attempts to understand Horace and his world, and to show the possibilities and the limits of our interpretations of him, the present book offers a critical exploration of his main works. The fragmentation of the poet's *œuvre* entailed by the assembling of separate contributors is unfair to Horace, but the method allows enthusiasts to write on what interests them most. The viewpoints are of course individual, but together they may be taken to represent current ways of approaching the poems. For practical reasons the coverage is not complete: the *Epodes, Carmen Saeculare* and *Epistles II* are not treated at length, but their omission does not imply their unimportance. The *Epodes* are of great interest as Horace's early experimental work; the *Carmen Saeculare* was a major landmark in his life – less important in itself than for what it symbolized in his poetic achievement; the second book of the *Epistles* contains much of his own mature views on literature.

In discussing the influence of Horace, whose impact on later literature is so pervasive and so elusive, one is well advised to do the job thoroughly and at length or not at all. Accordingly most of the contributors have been content to offer a few leads for the interested to pursue, while the final chapter is devoted entirely to Horace's reputation in England up to the seventeenth century, and concentrates on the many English translations which he inspired.

In the long run Horace speaks for himself, and those who befriend him are enriched. But new readers, especially in these days, can be helped to know him – as Byron regretted that he had not been helped to feel the Soracte ode – so that they may begin to understand why the grey-haired, quick-tempered little man, who liked the sun and wrote unique Latin poetry, has still after two millennia an unchallengeable place in European literature.

Abbreviations

AJP	American Journal of Philology
CP	Classical Philology
CQ	Classical Quarterly
CR	Classical Review
GR	Greece and Rome
JRS	Journal of Roman Studies
NQ	Notes and Queries
RE	Realencylopädie der classischen Altertumswissenschaft, ed. Pauly, Wissowa, etc., Stuttgart
Rh. Mus.	Rheinisches Museum
RSC	Rivista di Studi Classici
TAPA	Transactions of the American Philological Association

I

The Odes

Margaret Hubbard

Otium divos rogat in patenti
prensus Aegaeo, simul atra nubes
condidit lunam neque certa fulgent
    sidera nautis;
otium bello furiosa Thrace,
otium Medi pharetra decori,
Grosphe, non gemmis neque purpura ve-
    nale neque auro.
non enim gazae neque consularis
summovet lictor miseros tumultus
mentis et curas laqueata circum
    tecta volantis.
vivitur parvo bene, cui paternum
splendet in mensa tenui salinum
nec levis somnos timor aut cupido
    sordidus aufert.
quid brevi fortes iaculamur aevo
multa? quid terras alio calentis
sole mutamus? patriae quis exsul
    se quoque fugit?
scandit aeratas vitiosa navis
Cura nec turmas equitum relinquit,
ocior cervis et agente nimbos
    ocior Euro.
laetus in praesens animus quod ultra est
oderit curare et amara lento
temperet risu; nihil est ab omni
    parte beatum.
abstulit clarum cita mors Achillem,

longa Tithonum minuit senectus,
et mihi forsan, tibi quod negarit,
    porriget hora.
te greges centum Siculaeque circum
mugiunt vaccae, tibi tollit hinnitum
apta quadrigis equa, te bis Afro
    murice tinctae
vestiunt lanae: mihi parva rura et
spiritum Graiae tenuem Camenae
Parca non mendax dedit et malignum
    spernere vulgus.

(Ease is the prayer of the man caught on the open Aegean, as soon as a black cloud has hidden the moon and the stars fail to shine as certain guides to sailors, ease the prayer of war-mad Thrace, of the Medes whose ornament is the quiver, ease, Grosphus, that jewels and purple cannot buy, nor gold. For it is not eastern treasures nor the consul's lictor that clears the turbulent crowd of wretchedness of mind and the cares that flutter round coffered ceilings. A man lives well on little, if his father's salt cellar gleams on a frugal table and fear and low desire for gain do not steal his easy sleeps. Why in our short life do we strongly hurl our javelin at many marks? Why change for our own lands hot with another sun? Who in exile from his country has escaped himself as well? Flawed Care climbs aboard armoured ships and does not abandon squads of horsemen, swifter she than deer, swifter than the East wind as it drives the storm clouds. A mind cheerful for the present should reject caring about what is further on and water bitterness down with a mild smile; nothing is blessed in all respects. Swift-foot death stole glorious Achilles, long old age made Tithonus shrink, and to me perhaps, what she denies you, an hour will freely hand over. Round you a hundred flocks and Sicilian cows low, for you the mare fit for racing teams whinnies, you are dressed by wool twice dyed in African purple; for me a small estate and the delicate breath of the Greek Muse is the gift of the truthful Fate, and contempt for the crowd's malice.)

The impression that Horace's ode to Grosphus makes on a competent and cultivated reader demands analysis,[1] because the poem poses in a particularly sharp form some crucial problems about Horatian lyric. First and foremost, it is not obvious that a modern reader presented with a translation would recognize it as a poem at all, because of its formal and argumentative nature. Where is the poetic strangeness in 'A mind cheerful for the present should reject caring about what is further on and water bitterness down with a mild smile; nothing is blessed in all respects'? How is this moralizing not prose? Nor can this be put down to the deformations of translating. The Latin is equally disconcerting in the prosaic flavour of some of its terms, most notably those that refer to contemporary everyday features of real life (the consul's police escort *summovet* the crowds that get in a magistrate's way, *non summovet* the riotous cares that harry his mind). Indeed, to Horace's contemporaries such things must have been even more disconcerting than they are to us, as a central tradition of English poetry has always more easily accommodated the ordinary.

Yet equally no modern reader, even of a translation, could feel content with this as a piece of prose. The cows low, but what do the flocks do? Something equivalent to lowing. Flocks of what? Goats presumably, as wool is mentioned later, and this author, though he repeats sentiments, seems not to repeat images; two sets of sheep would be tedious. The lictor fails to clear a way through the crowd; Eastern treasures fail to perform a parallel but expressed service. The cares that at one moment were a riotous mob, at the next appear (though only by implication) as a swarm of bats, and then, by now singular, personified and turned into a hobgoblin, climbs armoured ships and does not desert squads of horsemen. *Otium* is first picturesquely identified as calm after storm and peace after war; only as the poem moves on do we find that these are images and that Horace is envisaging a different *otium*, the peace of mind that a man can secure for himself; at the end he shows himself in possession of an *otium* yet more exquisite, the withdrawn contentment of the poetic craftsman satisfied with his skill. But here the insistent repetitions of the earlier stanzas have been allowed to die away, and we are left to infer that the same concept is still involved; the actual word *otium* is in fact applied only to what Horace is not talking about. So though much is said, much is left to be inferred; for a descriptive statement in prose or for a prose statement of a moral position, too much.

3

And this is far from all. Such inferences as the preceding paragraph embodies could be made by any alert and intelligent reader; Horace has other demands still, and makes no concessions to those who think the truest aesthetic experience accrues to people who submit a poem to the *tabula rasa* of an uninformed mind. We shall not properly savour *abstulit clarum cita mors Achillem* unless we know that Death has stolen not merely Achilles but his standing epithet 'swift of foot', nor *longa Tithonum minuit senectus* unless our memory retains the echo of the plaintive cries Aphrodite describes to Anchises in the Homeric hymn (v.233 ff.):

> But when hateful old age entirely oppressed him and he
> could not move nor raise his limbs, the Goddess of Dawn
> decided this was the best plan: she settled him in his room
> and closed the bright doors. His voice flows on unceasing,
> nor is his former strength left in his twisted limbs. It is not
> in this way that I would have you immortal among the
> immortals.

'The delicate breath of the Greek Muse' is hardly even intelligible unless we know that *tenuis* proclaims adherence to a whole traditional programme of stylistic refinement and unless we can see what is implied by the fact that the Muse is given the epithet 'Greek' but called by her Roman name *Camena* (not *Musa*); this last elegancy cannot even be rendered into English in any tolerable way; its proud and confident acknowledgment of a debt due and paid escapes translation.

There is yet more: the poem expresses a dissent, by Horace's day itself conventional, from conventional Roman morality. Roman society, Roman intellectuals thought, was hostile to the life of the intellect; the claims of public and private duty kept the good citizen thoroughly engaged in business, *districtus negotiis* (*negotium* being the reverse of *otium*). Horace was to say himself that by contrast with Greece (*Epist.*, II.1.103 ff.):

> At Rome it was long a pleasure and the practice to wake
> early and open one's house, tell one's dependant his legal
> position, lay out cash on the guarantee of sound credit,
> listen to one's elders and tell one's juniors what would
> increase their capital and diminish their thriftless wantonness.

In such a society *otium* was suspect and Catullus had ruefully reproached himself with it, in lines that Horace deliberately echoes (51.13 ff.):

> otium, Catulle, tibi molestum est,
> otio exsultas nimiumque gestis;
> otium et reges prius et beatas
>   perdidit urbis.

(Ease, Catullus, is your bane, ease it is that makes you exultant and over-triumphant, ease before now has ruined kings and prosperous cities.)

The intelligentsia revolted: they were reproached as *otiosi*, but their *otium* was, they maintained, more valuable, even to their country, than the *negotium* of others. So Cicero defended in prefaces and letters the *otium*, enforced at that, that in two years gave Rome a great philosophical encyclopaedia in her own language. So Sallust (*Jugurtha*, 4.3 f.):

And I think that because I have decided to spend my time remote from politics some people will give my useful efforts the name of idleness, at any rate those who think it totally energetic to address the electorate by name and win influence by giving parties. If they reflect on the times when I won office, the sort of men who could not secure election then, the sort of men who *have* secured election since, they will surely realize that it is for good reason, not laziness, that I have changed my mind, and that my ease will produce more benefit to the state than others' business.

So, most subtly and obliquely, Virgil at the end of the *Georgics* contrasted his own *otium* with the achievements of Octavian in the war against Cleopatra:

> illo Vergilium me tempore dulcis alebat
> Parthenope, studiis florentem ignobilis oti,

writing, in fact, the *Georgics* in this inglorious retirement. Such are the resonances of the word Horace has chosen as the keynote of his ode. If we do not hear them, we miss much of his meaning.

Another piece of information helps too: Horace elsewhere tells us more about Grosphus, and what he tells us modifies the way we look at the poem. In 26 B.C. Horace had teased the young Stoic

Iccius for deserting philosophy to go on the Arabian campaign. Iccius had not made his fortune in Arabia (nobody did), but he had managed nicely for himself thereafter and in 20 B.C. was the manager of Agrippa's estates in Sicily, when Horace addressed an epistle to him (1.12), talking of Iccius' continued interest in philosophy and recommending Grosphus to him:

> verum seu piscis seu porrum et caepe trucidas,
> utere Pompeio Grospho et, si quid petet, ultro
> defer; nil Grosphus nisi verum orabit et aequum.
> vilis amicorum est annona, bonis ubi quid dest.

(But whether you're slaughtering fish or leek and onion, [2] make a companion of Pompeius Grosphus, and if he has any request, anticipate it; Grosphus will ask nothing that is not fair and just. The price of friends is cheap when it is good men who need something.)

Grosphus makes an agreeable appearance as a man of all seasons, virtuous and intelligent, a proper companion for the philosophic Iccius. So much the ode itself might have told us, if we are aware enough of the amenities of ancient encomiastic poetry to be sure that Grosphus is not being preached at and told to become a different sort of person or unfavourably contrasted with Horace; but confirmation of this common-sense generalization is welcome. [3] In either case, whether we proceed from Horace's characterization of Grosphus or from our knowledge of the encomiastic tradition, we need to know something outside the poem to be sure of getting it right.

Now there is no use blinking the fact that for an influential school of modern criticism a poet who demands this sort of exegesis to be intelligible is no poet. A distressed report by a teacher of English that the language of much English poetry was becoming unintelligible to people proposing to teach the subject in schools provoked a storm of fury at such intellectualism, of which the following may count as typical: [4]

> If certain passages of Milton cannot be really appreciated without presupposing a store of specialised knowledge in the reader, then they no longer qualify as poetry, being mere curios of interest only to inveterate booksniffers. Though little meaning remains for the modern reader in

classical and biblical references, he can yet accept them for what they are: elaborately structured mythologies, the attempt of other ages to give form to their own experience. Since it no longer touches some vital nerve, it seems highly pernicious to impose such an alien perspective on our children's view of poetry.

Horace is clearly subject to all these damnations; and the fact that the man was a wop writing in a foreign language and a dead one at that is certainly not going to make things better; for these latterday *marquis* he must be forbidden territory.[5]

Yet even if we are not much allured by the siren songs of self-canonized ignorance and believe that it is good for our imagination, not bad for our imagination, to put ourselves in unfamiliar stances and see what the world looks like from a point of view not our own, and believe even that such perspectives give a particularly acute pleasure, we may still have troubles of our own.

More precisely, when one has understood an Horatian ode on one level or another (I should not wish to deny that many are valid so far as they go), what is the nature of the pleasure one feels or should feel in it? First and foremost, of course, a straight sensuous one; Horace is one of the most harmonious of poets. But that is hardly going to win him readers in this day and age, where many of those who profess to like him best show a sadly defective ear for those harmonies. Verbal felicity is another matter. Most people who read Horace will not remain long unaware of the pleasures of his precise and chiselled language, of the way contrasts are sharpened and emphasized by juxtaposition, of the varying texture of his style, its economy and reticence. Yet this pleasure, though acute, is still fragmented; we are going to look for more in a whole poem than the exquisitely exact expression even of surprising thoughts. And many of Horace's thoughts are not surprising.

It is round about here that one comes to a particular difficulty of Horatian lyric and one that the Grosphus ode well illuminates. It would be hard to deny on the evidence of history that many people have admired, perhaps many still do admire, Horace for the same reasons that Patience Strong has been admired. Generations of the learned have nodded assent to Horace's sententious maxims, schoolmasters have inculcated them, statesmen quoted

them, men of all kinds found strengthening and consolation in
them. This is not necessarily quite wrong, though it tends to dis-
concert people with fashionable assumptions, at least in the West,
and though one can hardly assent with equal complacence to all
the maxims of the odes; some are incompatible. Horace himself
took pains to distinguish moral assent from poetic pleasure
(*Ars*, 333 ff.):

> aut prodesse volunt aut delectare poetae,
> aut simul et iucunda et idonea dicere vitae.
> quidquid praecipies esto brevis, ut cito dicta
> percipiant animi dociles teneantque fideles. . .
> centuriae seniorum agitant expertia frugis,
> celsi praetereunt austera poemata Ramnes:
> omne tulit punctum qui miscuit utile dulci,
> lectorem delectando pariterque monendo;
> hic meret aera liber Sosiis; hic et mare transit
> et longum noto scriptori prorogat aevum.

(Poets want either to do good or to give delight or to say
what is at once pleasurable and morally useful. Make all
your maxims brief, so that their speed makes men's minds
grasp them readily and retain them faithfully . . . The
centuries of the veterans harry what has no nourishment to
it, the lofty nobles pass by poems too acid in flavour; he
who mixes the useful and the sweet wins every vote,
delighting the reader and instructing him both together.
This is the book that earns its publishers money, this the
one that crosses the sea, makes its author known and extends
his life to the distant future.)

One can reasonably suppose that Horace would be discontented
if his readers did no more than note the vivid succession of
images in

> quid brevi fortes iaculamur aevo
> multa? quid terras alio calentis
> sole mutamus? patriae quis exsul
> se quoque fugit?

Even in the detail of such a stanza the moral sense is aimed at too,
and a total hostility to being done good to in this particular way

8

might at any rate diminish the possibility of taking pleasure in the poem, except on a fairly superficial level.

Still, even those who do not resist the notion of being morally improved by a poet (and why not by him, just as well as a weekly's leader writer?) can hardly but have misgivings about the notion that a poem can be made up of an elegantly expressed bundle of maxims of various provenance, however proved their utility. Something more organic seems needed, and in Horace's case this something is most often not provided by the suggestions of a contemporary scene and a personal passion, such as we have from the elegists, or by a specifically dramatic or narrative context such as Virgil gives us in the *Eclogues* or the *Aeneid*. And in consequence this something more organic has often been found in the attachment of the poems to the character and nature of the poet. It sometimes seems that critics would like to hold that, apart from virtues of form and expression, an Horatian ode or an Horatian epistle, not to mention an epode, has value not in itself but as rooted in and expressive of some stage in the development of Horace's personality.

This again is not necessarily quite wrong either, but it can have, has had, undesirable consequences in Horatian criticism, that make it necessary to consider what on earth Horace was up to in the *Odes*. The *Odes* have no real parallel in the ancient world, though they have a multiplicity of models, their themes and subject-matter a multiplicity of sources. What moved Horace to write them is in some respects a puzzle, and particularly what decided him to recreate the lyric of Alcaeus. Of course some weight can be given to the Roman desire for literary conquest; we can guess at but not really estimate the driving power of the passion that impelled them, alone of all the peoples who came in contact with the Greeks, to create a literature that, however dependent on Greek models, was not Greek. Something too can be attributed to the general habit of ζῆλος, the emulation of earlier writers, that was imposed by the educational system common by this time to both the Greek and the Roman world. Something, no doubt, to the desire for a peculiar excellence. In the *Satires* (1.10.40 ff.) Horace had, tongue in cheek, it is true (εἴρων γάρ), explained his motive for writing satire: comedy, tragedy, epic, bucolic were fields already occupied by contemporary poets of note, whereas

9

hoc erat, experto frustra Varrone Atacino
atque quibusdam aliis, melius quod scribere possem,
inventore minor . . .

(In this genre, where Varro of Atax and some others had
made fruitless attempts, I could write better, though inferior
to its creator [Lucilius] . . .)

The re-creation of the forms of ancient lyric, touched on but most
incompletely by some Alexandrian poets and by Catullus, gave
him a similarly clear run. Some Alexandrians had used the Lesbian
metres: the Aeolic poems of Theocritus and probably Melinno's
hymn to Rome show the kind of modification they introduced. In
particular Asclepiades had given his name to the Alexandrian
version of two favourite metres of Alcaeus, and some of his
elegiac epigrams show the influence of Alcaeus' subject-matter,
though in a different genre. So for a Roman poet of Horace's
interests the emulation of Alcaeus was not an unobvious enterprise.

In Rome itself Horace may have been anticipated by Catullus.
We know Catullus imitated Sappho, indeed in one poem translated her; perhaps he tried Alcaeus too. At any rate his poem (30)
in greater asclepiads starts with a line that looks like an Alcaic
'motto' of the kind with which Horace so often calls attention to
his models:

Alfene immemor atque unanimis false sodalibus . . .

(Alfenus, you who forget and betray your comrades who
share one mind . . .)

The line has no exact correspondent in the extant fragments of
Alcaeus, but no one would be surprised to find such a line on a
papyrus tomorrow; the sentiment is common enough, reminding
us especially of Alcaeus' reproaches to Pittacus for deserting the
aristocratic coterie. But if the first line of Catullus' poem recalls
Alcaeus, the second does not:

iam te nil miseret, dure, tui dulcis amiculi?

(have you by now in your cruelty no pity for your poor dear
friend?)

Not only the sentiment but the pointedly affecting tone of the very rare diminutive *amiculus* removes the line from any likely Alcaic context. Throughout the poem, indeed, what in the conceivable Alcaic model would have been an invective against political perfidy, becomes a reproach for the violation of a personal relationship; the plural *sodales* of the first line vanish and are replaced by the figure of Catullus alone, himself betrayed by the false promise of a beauteous day. Such a sentimentalizing and personalizing of the theme of betrayal is not unsophisticated, but it is not at all like Horace's dealings with Alcaeus. One would conjecture that it is not original in Catullus either; indeed in the political agonies of the dying republic it is perhaps less to be expected than a more direct exploitation of Alcaic topics. The mood is Alexandrian rather, and Catullus' immediate model perhaps Asclepiades, not Alcaeus.

Even if Catullus had anticipated Horace's relation to Alcaeus more than he seems to have done, the contrast between their poetic worlds is still marked. Horace was no more inclined than Virgil to reject the Alexandrian inheritance in poetry, the exploration and refined distinguishing of mood and attitude. But like Virgil he looked for a wider range than had contented the Alexandrians and their Roman heirs. In Alcaeus, as in Lucilius before him, he seems to have found a model for the expression or depiction of a complete personality deploying itself in diverse relationships (*Serm.*, II.1.30 ff.):

> ille velut fidis arcana sodalibus olim
> credebat libris, neque, si male cesserat, usquam
> decurrens alio, neque si bene; quo fit ut omnis
> votiva pateat veluti descripta tabella
> vita senis. sequor hunc . . .

(He beforetime entrusted his books, like faithful friends (*sodales*) with his secrets, not looking for any other outlet if things had gone wrong, or well; so that all of it is displayed, like a drawing on a votive tablet, all the old man's way of life. I follow *him* . . .)

> age dic Latinum,
> barbite, carmen,

Lesbio primum modulate civi,
qui ferox bello, tamen inter arma
sive iactatam religarat udo
    litore navim,
Liberum et Musas Veneremque et illi
semper haerentem puerum canebat
et Lycum nigris oculis nigroque
    crine decorum. (*Carm.*, 1.32.3 ff.)

(Come sing a Latin song, lyre first tuned by the citizen of
Lesbos who though brave in war yet in the intervals of
fighting or when he had tied up his storm-tossed ship from
the drenched shore, would sing of Bacchus and the Muses
and Venus and the lad always at her side and of Lycus
beautiful with his black eyes and black hair.)

Alcaeus was 'the citizen of Lesbos' and that was important: it
imposed duties and actions, a whole area of life that the Alexandrians did not share but that had engaged Horace in his vigorous
youth and from which he did not willingly retreat. There was also
Alcaeus the private person with passions and enthusiasms of his
own; here the analytic techniques of Hellenistic philosophy and
Alexandrian phenomenology gave the poet a new world of expression. For this reason a modern Alcaeus was bound to be a more
complicated and ambiguous creature than the original. But
Horace could with Alcaeus' help aim at a completeness the
Alexandrians had prudently eschewed. Horace expressed his
judgment sharply when in a poem, probably earlyish, he told how
he had almost been killed and seen in the underworld (*Carm.*,
II.13.24 ff.)

Aeoliis fidibus querentem
Sappho puellis de popularibus,
et te sonantem plenius aureo,
    Alcaee, plectro dura navis,
      dura fugae mala, dura belli.
utrumque sacro digna silentio
mirantur umbrae dicere; sed magis
    pugnas et exactos tyrannos
      densum umeris bibit aure vulgus.

(Sappho singing plaintively to the Aeolian lyre about the girls of her city and you, sounding a fuller strain with the golden plectrum,[6] Alcaeus, to tell of the hardships of seafaring, exile, war. The shades marvel that each tells what demands a holy silence; but the thronging crowd more avidly listens to battles and the expulsion of tyrants.)

The personal world of the affections was not the whole of life; but it was by now the most thoroughly explored in poetry. New ways of apprehending it could be exploited in other areas as well, and Alcaeus suggested a map of those areas. At the same time the lyric form, compressed and allusive, enabled much conflict to be held in tension that in the *Epistles*, for all their technical virtuosity, was to become fragmented.

An ode, not one of Horace's best, that nevertheless shows how Alcaeus could be useful to a poet with Horace's preoccupations and yet how entirely a theme he prompted had to be transformed, is I.14, the allegorized address to the ship of state.

> O navis, referent in mare te novi
> fluctus! o quid agis? fortiter occupa
>   portum! nonne vides ut
>   nudum remigio latus,
> et malus celeri saucius Africo,
> antennaeque gemant, ac sine funibus
>   vix durare carinae
>   possint imperiosius
> aequor? non tibi sunt integra lintea,
> non di quos iterum pressa voces malo.
>   quamvis Pontica pinus,
>   silvae filia nobilis,
> iactes et genus et nomen inutile,
> nil pictis timidus navita puppibus
>   fidit. tu, nisi ventis
>   debes ludibrium, cave.
> nuper sollicitum quae mihi taedium,
> nunc desiderium curaque non levis,
>   interfusa nitentis
>   vites aequora Cycladas.

(O ship, new waves will carry you out to sea again. O what are you doing? Make an effort and get into harbour in time.

Don't you see how your side is stripped of oars, your mast
wounded by the swift south wind, your yardarms groaning
and how without ropes your keels can hardly endure the
domineering sea? You have no untorn sails, no gods to call
on in this second disaster. Even though, a Pontic pine,
daughter of a wood of note, you boast a descent and name
that do no good, the terrified sailor puts no trust in painted
poops. You, unless you owe the winds a laugh, look out!
Not so long since the object of my distraught irritation, now
of fond longing and deepfelt concern, may you avoid the
seas that roll between the gleaming Cyclades.)

The storm at sea was, we know, used as an image for political
strife by Alcaeus,[7] 'to satiety' according to one ancient critic,
'quite sufficiently' says another more politely; economy was not
among the things Horace learnt from his literary forebear. Fragments of two extant poems are relevant, perhaps also a fragment of
a third. One poem suggested the *novi fluctus* and *fortiter occupa
portum*, the second the details of the damage suffered by the ship.
In a third a ship is compared to a worn-out prostitute (or a prostitute to a ship); that this veiled any further reference to political
faction is very doubtful, but it is the only instance in Alcaeus
where a ship is personalized as it is in Horace.[8]
   In the first of these poems the image motivates a vigorous
exhortation to his companions to show courage, in the second it
illuminates the desperate situation of Alcaeus and his friends:

I do not understand the direction of the wind; for one wave
rolls from one side, one from another, and we in their midst
are swept along with our black ship, toil-worn by the great
tempest.

In the third the plight of the ship, courtesan or faction is something that he prefers to forget in drink and conversation with
friends. Each of the poems involves a plural 'we' or 'you', the
poet and his companions in war, faction, symposia and seafaring.
No such society was available to Horace and he prudently refrains
here from any pretence that there was, leaving vague even
whether, like Alcaeus, he is on board the ship or an anguished
spectator on shore. In the conditions of Roman political life what
else was he to do? Alcaeus' strivings ended in failure but they

lasted throughout his life; Horace's brief season of glorious energy had been cut off years before at Philippi.[9] For Alcaeus' picture of dangers faced and shared he offers a painfully felt statement of renewed involvement and concern. An adult man in a complex society had only some points of contact with an aristocratic ruffian and freebooter six centuries older.

The form in which the new attitude is expressed is as remarkably changed as the content. Horace has here not even retained the original metre, substituting an Asclepiad stanza, the most fluent and lyrical of them, for the Alcaics in which all the relevant poems of Alcaeus are written. One other change of detail, characteristic of the practice of the Augustan poets, may be noted. Page points out that at one point Alcaeus develops his picture beyond any imaginable allegorical interpretation and adds:[10]

It may then be most prudent to conclude that Alcaeus' metaphor and Homer's simile have this feature in common: that, once begun, they may go their way without scrupulous regard for the context out of which they arose; the colours of the image are not all to be found in the original. The allegorical picture is drawn by Alcaeus not from pure imagination but from personal experience. He himself has weathered the tempests of the Aegean, and knows the nature of its perils; when he describes the plight of his comrades in terms of a storm at sea, he is prompted by vivid memories to include in his narrative details which are true to his experience, however doubtfully appropriate to his poetic theme.

This detail, of the poet's being saved from death only because his feet are tangled in ropes, Horace has suppressed and seems to have substituted for it one more relevant to his allegory: the ship has lost the images of the gods from its poop and now lacks their protection in this new danger. Such tightening of the application in imagery is not confined to Horace.[11]

More important is the fact that the whole poem is cast in the form of an address to the ship, a stylistic device we can hardly attribute to Alcaeus. It is true that in the third fragment mentioned above (p. 14) he attributes wants to the prostitute/ship, where someone unspecified says she no longer wants to fight the rains . . . but to strike on a hidden reef and . . .

True too that weapons in Homer are sometimes presented as sentient, 'eager to have their fill of flesh' and so on. But a different level of personification seems involved when the inanimate object is directly addressed and treated as responsive to human appeals, as it is at certain moments of high emotion in Attic tragedy, when the watchman hails the beacon that marks the end of his long waiting (Aesch., *Ag.* 22, ὦ χαῖρε λαμπτήρ), Alcestis assures the marriage-bed that is the cause of her death that she bears it no grudge (Eur., *Alc.* 177 ff., ὦ λέκτρον . . .), Philoctetes tells the bow, now stolen from him, how it will mourn its change of master (Soph., *Phil.* 1128 ff., ὦ τόξον φίλον . . .).[12] All of these use the affective ὦ and so does Horace here, with a power heightened by the comparative rarity of O in Latin.[13]

Of course the apostrophe is not merely a stylistic device. Throughout the poem, not merely at the end, Horace's attention is concentrated on the ship, not on Alcaeus' 'we'; whereas in Alcaeus the damage to the ship is detailed because of its effects on Alcaeus and his friends, in Horace the concern is for the ship itself, and the poet's own interest, one of feeling, not of individual danger, is reserved for the end and then expressed in the vocative case. Not however that we are in any doubt about it earlier on; but in the earlier part of the poem Horace's anxiety is voiced not directly but dramatically: it emerges from the tone and content of what he says to the ship, and the reader is left to make legitimate inferences, not just bluntly told what to think. The reader's perspective, that is, is other than the poet's; whereas the poet represents himself as totally intent on the ship, its danger and its condition, the reader looks at the relation between poet and ship.

When the poet does define his feeling in the last stanza, he uses terms from the language of love: *taedium, desiderium* and *cura* belong to the lover's vocabulary. The notion of being in love with one's city is a Greek one, eloquently urged by Pericles in the Funeral Speech and perhaps professed by him in actual fact;[14] it is not, so far as we can see, one entertained by or even likely in Alcaeus, but belongs to a later and more reflective society. More noteworthy still is the extreme precision and self-consciousness of Horace's description of his states of mind: *taedium* and *desiderium*, *sollicitum* and *cura* play against each other, economically but accurately delineating complex attitudes. *taedium* especially has more implications than show at first sight, and takes us further back in time: Horace had long since been in love with the ship, had fallen out of love, and is now in love again, with an anxious and protective affection. Such distinctness of feeling and critical awareness also presuppose the developed habit of reflection and psychological analysis; there is nothing like it in Alcaeus, nothing even in Sappho. Intently though she observed herself, such refinement of vocabulary and concepts was simply not then available.

In the light of this it is perhaps time to look back at II.16 and ask again what it is that gives the poem organic unity. Here too one can find that unity in the dramatic situation in which the personality of Horace confronts that of Grosphus, and particularly in the assumed identity of interests between them: philosophy, moral cultivation, the search for peace and delight of mind, these they share. Horace understands what it is to be Grosphus, a quiet man though rich, Grosphus what it is to be Horace, and the deep content of the artist who has his own approval. The reader is invited to contemplate this understanding, grasp these attitudes, apprehend these two meeting personalities, take pleasure particularly in the fact that in such society more can be implied than needs to be said. Here too, and in many other of the odes, the real picture that is being presented is not precisely what appears (Horace giving admonitions to Grosphus), but a dramatic one, Horace in conversation with another person whose own implied personality modifies what the poet says, subtly affects the facets of his own nature that he shows. The poet does display himself to us (at least as he chooses to be seen; we need not bother about the relation to reality); but he displays himself as it were in reflection after reflection, and the mirrors themselves are not the same as each other.

The dramatic nature of an Horatian ode does not always of course appear so obliquely as in the Grosphus poem. Like the elegists, Horace has some scene-setting opening lines that plunge one at once into a conversation that is assumed to be already going on. So Maecenas is asked if he is surprised that Horace, though a bachelor, is preparing a sacrifice on the matrons' feast day of 1 March (III.8), Asterie why she is weeping for Gyges (III.7), while Lyde's objections are removed with (III.28.1 ff.):

Festo quid potius die
Neptuni faciam? prome reconditum,
Lyde, strenua Caecubum . . .

(What else should I do on Neptune's feast day? Bestir
yourself, Lyde, and bring out the stored up Caecuban . . .)

Sometimes, less obviously, we are surprised when some hint later
in the poem shows us that we should all the time have been
imagining a scene and a situation. In II.11.13 ff., for instance, after
three stanzas urging on Hirpinus Quinctius the desirability of not
worrying about distant or future possibilities Horace proceeds

cur non sub alta vel platano vel hac
pinu iacentes sic temere et rosa
    canos odorati capillos,
        dum licet, Assyriaque nardo
potamus uncti?

(Why don't we under a tall either plane or this pine lie
down just as we are, and with roses scenting our white
hair, while we can, and perfumed with Assyrian nard, start
drinking?)

The affected casualness of the word order in l.13 sharply indicates,
as does *hac*, that Horace is and has been talking. A similar pointed
use of the demonstrative does the same job quite late in the ode to
Dellius (II.3.12): 'huc vina et unguenta . . .' and in that to Postumus (II.14.22): 'harum quas colis arborum . . .'.

Perhaps oftener than we can know, Horace's choice of imagery
and vocabulary is determined by the personality and interests of a
poem's recipient. Fraenkel pointed out something like this in
II.17, where Horace's assumption of credulity (though not much
credulity) about astrology is motivated by Maecenas' beliefs. The
same may be true of the fiery Chimaera and hundred-handed
Gyges of ll. 13 ff.; at any rate they find a parallel in the demonology, uncharacteristic of Horace, offered to another friend who
probably came from the borders of Etruria and Umbria, Postumus
(II.14).[15] There is not much likelihood that Horace's imagination
was touched by necrological monsters; the imagination of his
Etruscan friends is another matter. Similarly Tibullus is teased in
the standard imagery of the elegists in 1.33, Valgius by the use of

the neoteric topic of the identity of the morning and the evening
star, exemplified notably in his favourite poet, Cinna (II.9.10 ff.):[16]

> nec tibi Vespero
> surgente decedunt amores
> nec rapidum fugiente solem.

(and your love does not give way, either when Vesper rises
or when he puts the swift sun to flight.)

In the ode to Pollio Jugurtha makes a rather puzzling appearance
in a context where a conventional Roman would put Hannibal
(II.1.25 ff.):

> Iuno et deorum quisquis amicior
> Afris inulta cesserat impotens
> tellure victorum nepotes
> rettulit inferias Iugurthae.

(Juno and any god friendly to the Africans who, powerless
to help, had withdrawn from the land and left it unavenged,
duly paid the grandsons of the victors as a funeral sacrifice
to Jugurtha.)

The commentators mention that Metellus Scipio, one of the
republican generals defeated and killed at Thapsus, was the grand-
son of Metellus Numidicus who fought well, though with less
than total success, against Jugurtha. Perhaps we need not worry
that, for that matter, the aunt of the victor of Thapsus was the
wife of Marius, who actually did conquer Jugurtha. But it seems
at any rate more relevant to Pollio and his history, the subject of
the ode, that the Jugurthine war had been recounted by Rome's
greatest historian to date, the recently dead Sallust.[17]

It is important to be clear about the limits of the significance of
such phenomena, and of the investigations that bring them to
one's attention. Some such investigations turn out quite fruitless
for purposes of criticism: an inquiry into the life of Quintus
Dellius, for instance, though an entertaining study in itself, tells
us precisely nothing about the marvellous poem that Horace
wrote for him; the ode itself may suggest the inference that, like
other Romans of his kind, he constructed himself a family tree
going back to a mythical hero, Inachus, but that fact, if it is a fact,
is a fact about Dellius and Roman history, not about Horace's

ode. In this instance, indeed, as in some others where grave con-
solations and austere admonitions are addressed to persons whom
history shows to have been engagingly disreputable, attention to
their biography can either distract one's eye from the poem or
distort one's view of it. The ode to Plancus (1.7), for instance, has
been much mangled in interpretation because we know too much
about Plancus and most of what we know is not relevant.

In other cases the point of such probing is defensive merely, to
prevent one's getting a poem wrong: here one could often wish
that it were, as it should be, unnecessary. Common sense, not to
mention an ear alert to its exquisite harmonies, among the most
subtle and refined in all Horace, should be enough to make anyone
doubt, for instance, whether the ode to the poet C. Valgius (11.9)
can be adequately summed up in the phrases 'impatient rebuke',
'Horace berates him' and so on. But if it is not enough, then a
look at the elegant fragments of Valgius' own poetry and reflection on the fact that he was a friend whose judgment of poetry
Horace had valued for years can usefully change one's perspective.
Common sense, and a minimal respect for Horace's own sense and
tact, should also be enough to save him from the supposition that
in telling Sallustius Crispus (11.2) that 'silver has no colour while
hidden in the greedy earth' and in going on to urge the desirability
of taming one's avarice he was reproaching Sallustius for acquisi-
tiveness. If it is not, we shall be the better for remembering that
Bacchylides, in praising his princely patron, Hieron of Syracuse,
told how at his Olympic victory the crowd exclaimed (111.10 ff.)

> Ah! thrice blessed the man who knows . . . how not to hide
> his towering wealth in black-cloaked darkness,

and that Pindar addressed the same open-handed prince with the
words (*Pythian*, 1.90 ff.):

> If you want to have sweet good report for ever, be not
> over-weary in spending. Let out your sail to the wind like a
> helmsman. Be not deceived, my friend, by juggling gains.
> The boast of fame that lives after mortals alone points out
> the way of life of great men dead to chroniclers and poets.
> Croesus' friendly excellence does not fade . . .

and that a contemporary poet Crinagoras exalted Sallustius'
myriad kindnesses to his friends (*Anth. Pl.*, 40). In the same ode

the amiable Proculeius is praised for his fatherly affection to his brothers, and here common sense has the bad luck to be left on its own. It suggests that if Proculeius is praised in an ode addressed to Sallustius they are at the least on terms of close friendship, or even, what the terms of the praise rather suggest, close kin. Unfortunately no one tells us what Sallustius Crispus' name was before he was adopted under his great uncle's will, or in what, if any, relation he stood to Proculeius' much married mother. So Horace is exposed to the calumnious hypothesis that he praised Proculeius to dispraise Sallustius.[18]

Such a defensive use of external information is not quite all there is to it, however. In particular the last example directs one's attention to a Greek poet much greater than Alcaeus, and one for whom Horace felt a deeper kinship. Alcaeus gave him a form and a range of subject-matter; his themes could be exploited and outdone. Horace's regard for him, though enthusiastic, is untempered by awe. It was different with Pindar. His harmonies, with their marvellous flexibility, were not more than half comprehensible and certainly inimitable; the Alexandrians themselves, greatly though they admired him, made no attempt to refurbish his metres as they did those of the Lesbian and Ionian lyrists. In the *Epistles* Horace asked with affectionate politeness after a young contemporary, Titius, who had undertaken the imitation of Pindar; but he clearly thinks it likely that Titius has by now taken refuge in tragedy (1.3.9 ff.). He himself had too much sense to court the fate of Icarus, as he eloquently explains in *Odes* IV.2. The whole world that had made possible choral lyric of such complexity was long dead, and a Latin Pindaric would have been as unreal as and only less absurd than the English one.

But something of Pindar was nevertheless accessible. Horace read Pindar as Erasmus Schmid did and as we are again learning to do,[19] as the perfect master of the rhetoric of encomium, the poet who best knew how to adapt praise to the recipient of praise, and to direct to that purpose the most varied range of themes and examples. In his characterization of Pindar in IV.2 Horace's order is instructive:

> Monte decurrens velut amnis, imbres
> quem super notas aluere ripas,
> fervet immensusque ruit profundo
> Pindarus ore,

laurea donandus Apollinari,
seu per audaces nova dithyrambos
verba devolvit numerisque fertur
    lege solutis,
seu deos regesque canit, deorum
sanguinem, per quos cecidere iusta
morte Centauri, cecidit tremendae
    flamma Chimaerae,
sive quos Elea domum reducit
palma caelestis pugilemve equumve
dicit et centum potiore signis
    munere donat,
flebili sponsae iuvenemve raptum
plorat et viris animumque moresque
aureos educit in astra nigroque
    invidet Orco.

(Like a torrential mountain stream, fed beyond its banks by
rains, Pindar boils and rushes on in a flood of song
immeasurably deep, earning the prize of Apollo's bay,
whether in bold dithyrambs he rolls along new words and
sweeps on in rhythms unchecked by rule, or sings of gods
and kings, gods' kindred, at whose hands the Centaurs met a
just death, and the flame of the terrible Chimaera, or tells of
those the Olympic palm brings home exalted to heaven,
boxer or horse, and presents them with a gift outdoing a
hundred statues, or bewails the youth a weeping bride has
lost and raises his strength and spirit and character to the
stars, all gold, and grudges them to black Orcus.)

Horace seems to start from what he could not use and come nearer
and nearer to what he could. Dithyramb was inaccessible,
Pindar's hymn at any rate not the sort of hymn that Horace chose
to write; but praise and consolation were another matter. *Centum
potiore signis munere donat* was something Horace disclaimed in the
ode to Censorinus (iv.8); as lavish as Pindar he could not be, but
the gift he had to offer was not contemptible; he would like to give
precious statues to Censorinus and his other friends,

    sed non haec mihi vis, non tibi talium
    res est aut animus deliciarum egens.

gaudes carminibus; carmina possumus
donare, et pretium dicere muneri.

(But I have not that power, and not your estate and not your
mind need such delights; songs are your joy; songs I can
give, and put a value on my gift.)

It was only in a few poems that Horace tried to write something
that, though in the metrical forms of Lesbian lyric, had some
architectural similarity to a Pindaric ode; he failed in 1.12, over-
elaborating and over-anxiously modernizing and, above all,
missing concreteness, triumphantly succeeded in iv.4, where the
episode of the Metaurus gave him, from Rome's heroic age,
something that had the emotional and ennobling power of a
Pindaric myth. In a few more poems he explicitly treated Pindaric
themes, though sometimes putting them to very un-Pindaric purposes (in iii.4, for example). But the influence of Pindar was much
more pervasive; he provided a model of discourse, prompted a
fierce pride in craftsmanship. Far more than Alcaeus, he set
Horace a standard: that was how a poet of conscious power had
been able to talk to the world and particularly to the great. [20]

Yet if we think of Horace beside Pindar, something else
becomes apparent about Horace's involvement with his audience.
Though our understanding of Horace is imperfect unless we are
sensitive to his relation to his Greek predecessors, it is a mistake
to stop at the recognition of likeness. Even in his relation to
Pindar Horace exploits a convention and a tradition to create
something new and something Latin. In the case of a Greek parae-
netic or encomiastic poet it is not only uncalled for but illegiti-
mate to infer anything about what personality is being imputed to
the recipients of his poems. Their circumstances, family and
achievements may dictate the choice of myth, example or *sententia*,
but personality is an uncomprehended irrelevance, and even the
interests of the addressee rarely seem to determine a poem's movement. [21] The *laudandus* is not X being praised, but a prince, a
victor, a beautiful youth. And this is as true of Alexandria as of the
classical period: who could guess from Theocritus xvi and xvii
what differences, except of circumstances, there might have been
between Hieron II of Syracuse and Ptolemy? They are princes
and generous patrons of poetry, or at least Theocritus hopes so
(wrongly, apparently, in Hieron's case); Hieron is more warlike,

Ptolemy, not being the first of his line, shows a more exemplary piety in advertising the divine merits of his father and mother. That is all. But in Horace's case it is not only legitimate but necessary to ask what attitudes and what personality are being attributed to the person addressed, to try to read this from the poem, to reinforce it where we can by what else we can know. In the poetry of friendship and praise, as in the poetry of love, the Roman poet is not exclusively interested in himself. Horace himself provides a clue in his praise of Pindar's threnodies:

> viris animumque moresque
> aureos educit in astra . . .

This whole categorizing of people by the assortment of their qualities belongs not to Pindar but to a poetry that has assimilated the lessons of philosophy, that is, the poetry of the Augustan age; we hear in it not Pindaric threnody but the grave harmonies of Horace's own lament for Quintilius:

> ergo Quintilium perpetuus sopor
> urget. cui Pudor et Iustitiae soror,
> incorrupta Fides, nudaque Veritas
>   quando ullum inveniet parem?
> multis ille bonis flebilis occidit,
> nulli flebilior quam tibi, Vergili . . .

(So the everlasting sleep imprisons Quintilius. When will Modesty and Justice's sister, incorruptible Loyalty, and naked Truth ever find his peer? Many good men have cause to weep for his death, none more than you, Virgil . . .)

It is in this sense that one can justify the feeling that the significance of the *Odes* depends partly on their being rooted in personality, though not in the personality of Horace, which remains perpetually elusive. In poem after poem Horace creates a world of characters, discovering or imputing tastes, interests, moral and intellectual attitudes; it is perhaps because individual poems so often strike us as fragments of this world that the temptation to look for their justification outside them has been so strong. But if in thus looking outside the individual poems we seek their justification either in the real personality of Horace or in the real personality of his friends and patrons, we are looking in the wrong direction. For it remains strictly irrelevant whether those friends were as he represents them or not; or rather, with rare exceptions,[22] we can be sure they were not so civilized, tactful, humorous, so quick to grasp the bearing of an *exemplum*, to catch an allusion to the images and topics of poetry, often obscure, and of philosophy. Horace's problem was like that of Cicero when he wrote his philosophical works: the fit audience to listen to what he had to say did not exist, and the author had to create it, first in imaginative presentation, hoping thus to cajole and flatter it into real existence.[23]

The society of Rome was nasty and brutal, bloody and immersed in business. A generation earlier Lucretius had expressed the dilemma of the philosophic poet in his opening prayer to Venus (1.29–30, 41–3):

> effice ut interea fera moenera militiai
> per maria ac terras omnis sopita quiescant. . . .
> nam neque nos agere hoc patriai tempore iniquo
> possumus aequo animo nec Memmi clara propago
> talibus in rebus communi deesse saluti.

(See to it that meantime the savage offices of soldiering are drugged and sleep on every land and sea . . . For I cannot attend to this undistracted while my country's state is critical nor can Memmius' glorious scion in such times fail the common weal.)

He had moreover frankly told Memmius that and how he hoped to improve him (1.943 ff.):

> sic ego nunc, quoniam haec ratio plerumque videtur
> tristior esse quibus non est tractata, retroque
> vulgus abhorret ab hac, volui tibi suaviloquenti
> carmine Pierio rationem exponere nostram
> et quasi musaeo dulci contingere melle,
> si tibi forte animum tali ratione tenere
> versibus in nostris possem, dum perspicis omnem
> naturam rerum qua constet compta figura.

(So I now, since most people who have not dealt with it think this system rather harsh to the taste, and the vulgar shrink from it, have chosen to set out our system for you in the sweet-voiced song of the Muses and to touch everything with the sweet honey of poetry, in the hope that in this way I can keep your attention fixed on my verses, until you perceive the whole nature of things, its shape and arrangement.)

Horace's sympathy with the great poet who had made an Epicurean of him, as he made an Epicurean of Virgil and others of the choicest spirits of the age, was and remained profound, but his technique was more insinuating and less downright. To Roman society as it was he held up a mirror in which it could see a pattern of civility; and because in his suggestions of character and personality he ranged so wide and offered a picture so varied and refined in detail, he still holds that mirror up to us.

Notes

1 One must add this qualification, because what an incompetent and uncultivated reader might make of it is literally unimaginable. The competent and cultivated may console themselves with the reflection that it was certainly for them that Horace was writing.

2 This transitional phrase makes two points. Horace had mentioned Iccius' interest in Empedocles, and Empedocles, who believed in the transmigration of souls, forbade the eating of fish and meat, while some Egyptian religions banned leek and onion; Iccius' intellectual allegiances are therefore in question. But it is also relevant that seafood was a characteristic ingredient of sumptuous banquets as against the vegetarian diet of devotees of the simple life; so possible styles of living are also envisaged.

3 See further above, p. 20.

4 *The Sunday Times*, 13 February 1972. If the author of this particular effusion was being ironical, I apologize. The trouble is that in this area parody is strictly undetectable.

5 *Que sais-je, moi? je ne me suis pas seulement donné la peine de l'écouter. Mais enfin je sais bien que je n'ai jamais rien vu de si méchant, Dieu me damne . . .*

6 The golden plectrum normally belongs to Apollo or the Muses; presumably the instrument is also his, the great concert *cithara*, as distinct from Sappho's simple lyre.

7 It is misleading to speak of Alcaeus as using the image of the 'Ship of State'; he hardly has the concept of the state, and all the poems seem to be talking about the fortunes, not of Mytilene, but of Alcaeus' own *hetaireia*. Theognis may already have some more organic society in mind (671 ff.); more important for later thinking is the developed scrutiny to which Plato subjected the image in the *Republic* (488).

8 A reference to political faction used to be supposed, before an ancient commentary was discovered, which points out the comparison with the prostitute. It is unlikely that Horace, who no doubt read his Alcaeus with a commentary, got this wrong; the most he could owe to Alcaeus here is the notion of personalizing the ship, but he may not owe even so much. The three fragments are fully discussed in Denys Page, *Sappho and Alcaeus*, Oxford, 1955, pp. 179 ff.

9 Even in recalling that period, when in 11.7 he celebrates the return to Rome of his friend Pompeius, he is discreet in his use of Alcaic themes. Pompeius and he had fought together under Brutus, and Pompeius was 'the foremost of my *sodales*;' but that relation is at once defined as convivial, not political. Alcaeus in welcoming home his brother Antimenidas had a particular exploit to praise, Antimenidas' killing of a Babylonian giant. Pompeius' activities since Philippi are hinted at merely: 'you the wave sucked back into war and carried you off on its turbulent flood'. The image may be appropriate to the fact if Pompeius joined Sextus; but the prudent vagueness of Horace's picture is worth noting.

10 *Sappho and Alcaeus*, p. 189.

11 For Virgil's practice in his similes cf. David West, *JRS* 59 (1969), pp. 40 ff.

12 This last example is still guarded by a condition which shows that the figure was felt as strange ('Oh dear bow, . . . surely, *if you can feel*, you see with sorrow that . . .').

13 So far as ships go, it is the innovating Timotheus, not Aeschylus, who reproaches the Greek fleet with the destruction of the Persians (791.178 ff.), while Callimachus later, in a passage Horace recalled in 1.3, addressed a ship that was carrying a friend from him (fr. 400); the fact that the fragments is in greater asclepiads cannot be used to show the figure was Alcaic.

14 Gomme cites the hypothetical speech in Aristophanes' *Knights* (1341 f.): 'O People, I am your lover and your friend, and I alone care for you and take counsel for you.'

15 That demonology is at one point unusual. Horace here, like Virgil in *Aeneid*, vi.289, puts Geryon in the underworld; no other writer does so, nor any Greek visual artist that we know of. A Greek literary source is of course postulated and may well have existed; but what is certain is that Geryon appears in the underworld, along with Sisyphus and Hades, in the later chamber (about 200 B.C.) of the Tomba dell' Orco at Tarquinia.

16 Cinna, fr. 6, 'te matutinus flentem conspexit Eous,/te flentem paulo vidit post Hesperus idem'; Valgius, fr. 2, 'And Codrus sings in such a voice as you used to sing and repeats your harmonies, Cinna, so that no sweeter strain flowed from the mouth of Pylian Nestor nor from Demodocus' poetic brain.'

17 The fact that Pollio, a cross-grained detractor from the merits of all his predecessors, may not have relished the implied compliment, only shows that circumstances could set limits to the success even of Horace's tactful praise.

18 The misinterpretation was put forward by a scholar apparently so ignorant

of Latin that he thinks there is something fishy about editors' insistence that *regnes* in l. 9 means 'One is king' (not 'You would be but aren't'), and so really ignorant of Horatian scholarship that he is surprised to find Bentley defending a manuscript reading. It would not be worth refutation if it had not found in Sir Ronald Syme at least one supporter who should know better. Sallustius himself, we are told, is not meant to understand the criticism; but the circle of Maecenas do recognize it and nudge each other with knowing giggles. Such attitudes belong to newspaper columns and commonrooms, not to ancient lyric.

19 Elroy L. Bundy's two monographs on Pindar's encomiastic technique have much to offer readers of Horace as well ('Studia Pindarica', Parts I and II, *Univ. Calif. Publ. in Class. Phil.*, 1962, 18, pp. 1–34, 35–92).

20 Of course there is more to it than that; it is particularly relevant that to a poet steeped in Callimachus Pindar was likely to be especially congenial. Newman's useful list of the points of contact between Pindar and Callimachus could be turned with very little alteration into a list of the points of contact between Pindar and Horace (J. K. Newman, *Augustus and the New Poetry*, Brussels, 1967, pp. 45 ff.).

21 Perhaps only in *Olympian* 2 can we be pretty sure of any such thing: the interest in an oddish eschatology is surely that of the Sicilian Theron, not of Pindar.

22 The principal exceptions are, one hopes, the poets. It would be too despairing to believe that Virgil did not understand 1.3 and iv.12, Varius 1.6, Tibullus 1.33, Valgius ii.9. Horace added Maecenas, perhaps not quite untruly; Maecenas' taste is after all vindicated by his substantial investment.

23 Cicero's difficulties in finding any set of Romans to whom he could plausibly attribute the discussions of the *Academica* vividly illustrate his problem (*Att.*, xiii.16.1, xiii.19.5); his final solution (himself, Atticus and Varro) shows an understandable loss of nerve. He came to lie more boldly, to the extent of presenting *Hirtius noster, consul designatus*, as eagerly demanding to be told the really rough stuff of the *de fato*.

II

Horace's Poetic Technique in the Odes

David West

The English-reading student in 1973 is well-placed to study Horace's poetic technique. He might start with the work of Gordon Williams,[1] particularly helpful on Horace's originality and the organization of the *Odes*. He should then move to Nisbet and Hubbard's[2] massive commentary on the first book, which raises and solves a vast range of problems and abundantly deploys the common store on which Horace drew. This chapter will enter the still exhaustless mine of contemplation by a different shaft, narrow and hazardous. We shall start from a small point of technique and show that it is frequent and important in the *Odes*; then study some apparent examples of this technique in the hope of improving our understanding of the passages where it occurs or seems to occur; then gather our observations to present a general picture of Horace's poetic technique in the *Odes*.

Aeneas is *blazing* as he sinks his sword in Turnus' breast, but the limbs of Turnus are loosened with *cold* ((*Aeneid*, XII.951):

> feruidus; ast illi soluuntur frigore membra.

Norden[3] is astounded at this last ornament by contrast in the *Aeneid*. It is the last of many. Collinge[4] examines such contrasts in Horace's *Odes* in his stimulating first chapter and shows that 'the setting off of A against B is the major motif of Horatian verbal composition'.

It takes many forms: oxymoron (*audaces agnos*, III.18, *inaudax raptor*, III.20, *palluit audax*, III.27); antitheses (*hac Dorium illis barbarum*, *Epodes*, 9.6), often of some complexity (III.12.10–12):

> catus idem per apertum fugientis agitato
> grege ceruos iaculari et celer arto latitantem
> fruticeto excipere aprum.

(He is shrewd at spearing stags when the herd of deer/is alarmed and flying over the open plain, and swift/to receive the boar hiding in the undergrowth.)

The symmetry of this formidable quintuple antithesis is relieved by minute variations: *celer* is the precise counterpoise to *catus*, but *per apertum* is different in form from *arto fruticeto*; *agitato grege* is an extra in the first colon but similar in form to *arto fruticeto* in the second; *fugientis* comes after *per apertum*, but *latitantem*, its counterpoise, is cunningly contained within *arto fruticeto*; in a final flourish 'the stags to spear' is set in chiasmus against 'to meet the boar'. After this fanfare we may look back and wonder why cunning is prized in the chase and speed in the ambush.

Sometimes these symmetrical structures contribute so much to the poetry that commentators can fairly be faulted for ignoring them. In 1.13 the antithesis is triple (1.13.1–4):

> cum tu, Lydia, Telephi
> ceruicem roseam, cerea Telephi
> laudas bracchia, uae meum
> feruens difficili bile tumet iecur.

(When you Lydia, praise Telephus's/rosy neck, and Telephus's/ waxen arms, oh my liver boils/and swells with bile it can't contain.)

There the counterpoint between the line endings and the shape of the antitheses leads us towards the balancing items: the derisive repeat of *Telephi*; the colour contrast highlighted by the juxtaposition of *roseam* and *cerea*; and, most important of all for the sense of the poem, the placing of *tu* and *meum*, amounting to a dramatic direction to the reader.

Antithesis in this essay, like *contentio* in *Rhetorica ad Herennium* and in Quintilian, is taken to mean balanced contrast. Contrast without balance is more difficult to name (Schuster[5] calls it 'Nebeneinanderstellunggegensätzlicher Begriffe'), but even more frequent in the *Odes*. For example, contrasting terms are juxtaposed in each of the first four *Odes – partem solido, aequore dammae, fragilem truci, soluitur acris*: the hedonist spends part of his whole day at his pleasures; the deer are at sea; the boat is fragile, the sea is grim; winter was frosty, now it is thawing. But often the trick goes deeper, as in 1.15.1–2:

> pastor cum traheret per freta nauibus
> Idaeis Helenen perfidus hospitam

where treachery clashes with the hostess; where the shepherd
betrays his calling by plundering, and is out of his element at sea
on board ship; where *Idaeis Helenen* offers the standard contrast of
nationalities which we have already seen in *Epodes*, 9.6 and which
Horace so often uses in describing his own achievement in setting
Latin poetry to Greek metres. *Dic Latinum, barbite, carmen* (1.32)
and *Aeolium carmen ad Italos* (III.30) are the same device and the
same claim.

Polar tension is often relevant to the argument of a poem. The
first ode of the second book is concerned with Pollio and his
history of the civil wars until the last stanza (II.1.37–40):

> sed ne relictis, Musa procax, iocis
> Ceae retractes munera neniae;
> mecum Dionaeo sub antro
> quaere modos leuiore plectro.

(But O my immoral Muse, don't give up your fun,/don't
take to the task of producing dirges like Simonides:/come
with me to the cave of Venus/and look for tunes that suit a
lighter plectrum.)

'The horrors of the past', writes Fraenkel,[6] 'seem to have faded
away; in the gentle finale we are watching a scene of sheltered
peace.' We are watching also a point-by-point refusal to write like
Pollio. Pollio's Muse of severe tragedy is briefly to desert the
theatre (*paulum seuerae Musa tragoediae desit theatris*, 9–10); Horace's
immoral Muse is not to abandon her frolics; she is to be with him
in the grotto of Venus; not in the tragic theatre, and not coping
with sterner divinities (*Iuno et deorum quisquis amicior Afris*, 25–6);
Pollio is engaged in matters of weight and substance; but *grauis*
(3), *plenum* (6) and *grande* (11) are answered by *leuiore*; so *tractas* (7)
by *retractes*; *coturno* (12) the tragic boot, by *plectro*; the *munus* of
tragedy (11) by the *munera* of Simonides; *repetes* (12) by *quaere*;
Pollio is concerned with *ludum Fortunae* (3); Horace's Muse is not
to give up her *iocis*; Pollio is concerned with *belli modos* (2);
Horace's Muse with a different kind of *modos*. If *Dionaeo* and *Ceae*
could be held to be counters to *Cecropio* (12), every word in the
last stanza (except *sub*) is in polar tension with at least one word in

the body of the ode. 'Better without', wrote Landor in his margin opposite this stanza, and without this stanza Horace would have written a nobler poem, but nobility is only one of Horace's targets. This student might find six such points of contrast in the last two lines of III.1, and many too at the end of II.16 and II.17, and in other modest disavowals by this poet.[7]

But similar contrasts occur in many different contexts (II.14):

> Eheu *fugaces*, Postume, Postume,
> labuntur anni nec pietas *moram*
> rugis et *instanti* senectae
> adferet *indomitaeque* morti,
> non si trecenis quotquot eunt dies,
> amice, *places inlacrimabilem*
> Plutona tauris, qui ter *amplum*
> Geryonen Tityonque tristi
> *conpescit unda*, scilicet omnibus,
> quicumque *terrae* munere uescimur,
> enauiganda, siue *reges*
> siue *inopes* erimus *coloni*.
> frustra *cruento* Marte carebimus
> fractisque *rauci* fluctibus Hadriae,
> frustra per autumnos nocentem
> corporibus metuemus Austrum.
> *uisendus ater* flumine *languido*
> Cocytos errans et Danai genus
> *infame* damnatusque *longi*
> Sisyphus Aeolides laboris.
> *linquenda* tellus et domus et *placens*
> uxor, neque harum, quas colis, arborum
> te praeter *inuisas* cupressos
> ulla *breuem* dominum sequetur.
> *absumet* heres Caecuba dignior
> *seruata* centum clauibus et mero
> tinguet *pauimentum superbo*,
> pontificum potiore cenis.

(Alas Postumus, Postumus, the gliding years are in flight/and devotion cannot block the pursuit/of wrinkles, old age and irresistible death: –/no my friend, not if you sacrificed three hundred bulls a day/to appease this pitiless god of the

underworld,/who confines the triple-vast Geryon/and Tityos/
within the river which we know must be crossed/by all who
feed upon the bounty/of earth, kings/and poor tenant-farmers
alike./In vain we shall avoid the bloody god of battle/and
the roaring breakers of the Adriatic,/in vain in the autumn
we shall worry/about unhealthy winds from the South;/we
must all go to the dark, sluggish, winding river/of Cocytus,
to the notorious daughters/of Danaus, to Sisyphus son of
Aeolus,/condemned to his long labour./You must leave
behind your land and your home/and the wife you love, and
none of your trees/will follow their short-lived owner/bar
the cypress which you hate./Your heir, a better man than
you, will go through/the Caecuban you have locked behind a
hundred keys/and the proud vintage, too good for a priest's
banquet,/will dirty the marble paving.)

'The first half of this poem', according to Nisbet,[8] 'falls short of
greatness, for though the words are solemn and sonorous, they
make no clear picture.' Williams[9] is equally in the dark with the
ticking away of time and the approach of death. There is a perfectly clear picture in this stanza and there are no approaches or
clocks. Polar tension is often a useful key to the force of a metaphor, and not only in Horace. A simple example will demonstrate
the method. 'Ac per hos dies libentissime otium meum in
litteris colloco quos alii otiosissimis occupationibus perdunt',
writes Pliny (*Epistles*, IX.6) – 'During these days with immense
satisfaction I invested my idle time in literature while others were
squandering theirs in utterly idle occupations.' For *colloco* the
translators offer 'devote' or 'fill' and the commentators have
nothing. But in this heavily antithetic author, *colloco* balancing
perdunt must have a financial connotation. By a similar *e sequentibus
praecedentia*,[10] *fugaces* in *Odes*, II.14 is to be understood in the light
of *moram* and each of these words in the light of the two contrasting words that follow, *instanti* and *indomitae*. The years are on the
run, old age and wrinkles are pressing them hard, death is invin-
cible, devotion cannot stop any of the three of them. The picture
is clear. It is a battle scene, a rout, vivid and precise.

In the second stanza, *places* and *inlacrimabilem* are in tension,
'placate the pitiless'. So *ter amplum* and *compescit*, 'confine the
triply vast'.[11] *Terrae* speaks to *unda*, 'all who feed upon the earth

DAVID WEST

must cross the wave'. The *coloni* are *inopes* as opposed to the *reges*.
Stanzas 4–6 comprise a triple triad. Three things we shall avoid in
vain(*frustra . . . frustra*). Three things we must visit (*uisendus* first in
the stanza). Three things you must leave behind you (*linquenda*
first in the stanza). Mars is bloody, but Cocytus is black. The
breakers of the Adriatic are noisy, but Cocytus is winding and
languid, and both form a counterpoise to the land you must leave
behind. The daughters of Danaus are infamous because they
murdered their husbands on the wedding night. How different
from the wife who pleases you, and she again from the cypresses
you hate. Sisyphus is condemned to long labour in the underworld. The owner of the trees is short lived. In the last stanza, the
Caecuban is laid down behind a hundred locks, but your heir will
drink it all. As a last juxtaposition of opposites *pauimentum superbo*
vividly suggests that the highest pride will be laid low.[12]

Is polar tension too frequent in this ode? Is it a sign of routine
work? Certainly not. Rather the varied contrasts between so many
details lend a characteristically Horation density to the thought.
Collinge[13] says that the ode 'almost looks like a *cento* of Horation
commonplaces . . . The four stanzas simply say that death has no
regard for (1) character, (2) offerings, (3) status, (4) evasive action.'
Our study of the contrasts, which are only a tiny part of what is in
the ode, suggests that such paraphrases have the same use as the
man in the foreground of the photograph of the Eiffel Tower.

The italics in the text of II.14 show at a glance that in this ode
at least, 'the setting off of A against B is the major motif of
Horatian verbal composition.' One last example may illustrate the
convenience of this pattern of thought (III.4.13–16):

> . . . mirum quod foret omnibus,
> quicumque *celsae nidum Aceruntiae*
> *saltusque* Bantinos et *aruum*
> pingue tenent *humilis* Forenti,

(. . . a miracle to all who live/in the lofty nest of Aceruntia,/
the pastures of Bantia and the rich tilth/of low-lying
Forentum,)

Celsae Aceruntiae is in explicit contrast to *humilis Forenti*, and
between these two *saltus Bantinos* provides a further diversification:
Aceruntia (833 metres above sea-level), a bird's nest on its hill-top

34

(Cicero had already used the image, *De Orat.*, 1.196); and from crag to pasture, Bantia (570 metres) high among its grassy valleys; and from pasture to arable, *aruum pingue humilis Forenti* suggesting in this context an alluvial plain, although Nissen[14] has to resort to assumptions to bring it down to 462 metres. When Horace is looking for three villages from his own part of the world to canonize in Aeolian verse, his main criterion of choice and the main characteristics celebrated are contrasting contours and contrasting land use. This tells us something about his technique and about his imagination. It is confirmed seven lines later when we read *arduos Sabinos* and *Tibur supinum*. This motif is so frequent that it might be called a formula for the provision of ornamental epithets. Poets using this formula would be in constant danger of falling into a mechanical reproduction of vacuous patterns. Not so Horace, or not often so. If we observe such contrasts in the *Odes*, we are led to a keener sense of the genius responsible for them. They demonstrate rather the richness of his dramatic sense, his visualization, his imagery and his tone of voice.

Contrasts and dramatic sense

Neu uiuax apium neu breue lilium (*Odes*, 1.36) may look like slack writing. Celery keeps fresh for some time; lilies wilt. *Ergo* two epithets from the machine, *uiuax* and *breue*. But this is not a generous view of the line. We are at a banquet of lovers. The contrast in expectation of life of the two vegetables is adding a dimension to the talk of love. The antithesis broadens the dramatic purchase of the poetry; it is not just a rhetorical carbuncle. There is however another passage where the drama does seem to labour (IV.9.19–28):

> . . . non pugnauit *ingens*
> Idomeneus Sthenelusue solus
> dicenda Musis proelia, non *ferox*
> Hector uel *acer* Deiphobus *grauis*
> excepit ictus pro pudicis
> coniugibus puerisque primus.
> uixere *fortes* ante Agamemnona
> multi; sed omnes inlacrimabiles
> urgentur *ignotique* longa
> nocte, carent quia uate sacro.

(... Neither huge Idomeneus nor Sthenelus has been alone/in
fighting battles worthy of the voice/of the Muses; neither
fierce Hector/nor deadly Deiphobus has been the first/to
suffer heavy blows in the defence/of their children and chaste
wives./Brave men have lived before Agamemnon in great
numbers, but all of them unwept/and unknown are crushed
in endless night/because they have no divinely inspired poet.)

ingens, ferox, acer, grauis, the intensives roll on a little too repeti-
tively, until the poem is saved by its great climax in *fortes* and the
annulling contrast *ignoti.* If this fails, it fails because of an abuse
not of contrast, but of hyperbole, the besetting failure of the
Aeneid.[15]

There are other passages in the fourth book of the *Odes,* where
poetry is degenerating into rhetoric.

'There is hardly anything in the *Odes* that can be called ornamen-
tation: *Ode* III.16.1–8 is most unusual in that every noun has an
adjective (most of them merely ornamental) which is placed next
to it.' So says Williams, and he finds these adjectives 'the one
serious weakness of the composition'.[16]

> *Inclusam* Danaen turris *aenea*
> *robustaeque* fores et *uigilum* canum
> *tristes* excubiae *munierant* satis
>   nocturnis ab adulteris,
> *si non* Acrisium uirginis *abditae*
> custodem *pauidum* Iupiter et Venus
> risissent: fore enim *tutum* iter et *patens*
>   conuerso in pretium deo.

(Shut in her tower of bronze, Danae/had been well enough
secured from night callers/by stout doors,/by savage and
unsleeping watch dogs/if Jupiter and Venus had not made a
mockery/of her nervous guardian Acrisius./They knew a safe
and open road – /turn the god into his fee.)

Far from being a weakness of this composition, the accumulation
of epithets gives it its dramatic force. *Inclusam* vigorously states
the theme and each of the next four adjectives increases the
apparent security of Danae, *aenea, robustae, uigilum, tristes;* and
munierant contributes the finality of the indicative mood – 'they

actually had protected her', – all forming a great enceinte breached with absurd ease by the two little words at the beginning of the next stanza – *si non*. *Abditae* and *pauidum* then characterize the nervous precautions taken by Acrisius to preserve his daughter's chastity. *Tutum* makes nonsense of the second, *patens* of the first, a splendidly satirical lead-in for the shock in the crowning epigram, where Jupiter is turned, not as expected into a shower of gold, but into payment for services rendered. This paraphrase is meant to show that nine of the epithets in this extract are in polar tension and that all go to shape a nicely judged dramatic movement. The tone is sardonic. Fraenkel's 'frigid allegory'[17] and Williams' 'poetic mystery'[18] are equally wide of the mark.

Contrast and visualization

The clash of colours is a stock device of Latin verse. Norden collects more than a dozen examples from the sixth book of the *Aeneid* in his note on ll. 9–10, and Virgil offers many other examples, some of them, like his description of the Nile, as weird as the temperature contrast with which this chapter began (*Georgics*, IV.293–1):

> usque *coloratis* amnis deuexus ab Indis,
> et *uiridem* Aegyptum *nigra* fecundat harena

(the river flowing down from the coloured Indians,/and fertilizes green Egypt with its black sand)

Such devices are equally common in the *Odes* of Horace. Enough to cite III.27.19–20 with *ater* and *albus* at the end of succeeding lines and 1.7.15–21, where two examples occur in one sentence ('albus *ut* obscuro' and '*seu* fulgentia *castra tenent seu* densa *tenebit* umbra'). This casts a glimmer of light on the famous epigram (III.1.38–40):

> neque
> decedit *aerata* triremi et
> post equitem sedet *atra* Cura.

We have all seen the dark figure seated behind the horseman. But a brass-plated ship will sparkle in the Mediterranean sun. *Aerata* is in tension with *atra*. We must see also the dark figure against the glittering trireme.[19] And if this is how Horace works we must look again at (II.16.21–2):

> scandit *aeratas uitiosa* nauis
> Cura nec turmas equitum relinquit

(Tarnished Care boards the ships of brass/and cleaves to the cavalry squadrons).

The brass plating on a rich man's ship is a manifestation of power, and *uitiosa* obviously suggests the corruption which attends upon it. But apart from this moral observation, we are led also to a material visualization. The panoply gleams in the sun and *uitium* is the tarnishing of the brass.

It may support this suggestion to notice that Horace often uses the word *sordidus* in the *Odes* with a contrast between the dull and the brilliant. In II.1, after the flashing armour, Horace imagines the great leaders soiled but not disgraced by dust ('fulgor *armorum, non indecoro puluere* sordidos'). In II.16 the family salt-cellar gleams on the table and sordid lust doesn't carry off light sleep ('splendet *salinum nec levis somnos cupido* sordidus *aufert*'). In III.2 virtue knows nothing of the squalor of electoral defeat but shines with honours unsullied ('repulsae *nescia* sordidae *intaminatis* fulget honoribus'). In IV.11.11 the flames are spinning the dirty smoke ('sordidum *fumum*', ll. 10–11) as opposed to the smiling of the silver ('ridet *argento domus*') and the brilliant beauty of Phyllis, (ll. 5–6).[20]

Another visualization is clearly indicated by a multiple antithesis (1.35.21–6):

> te Spes et albo rara Fides colit
> uelata panno nec comitem abnegat,
>   utcumque mutata potentis
>   ueste domos inimica linquis,
> at uolgus infidum et meretrix retro
> periura cedit

(Hope and that rare visitant Honesty,/draped in holy white, attend you,/and stay with you when you change your dress/ and leave the rich man's house in displeasure./But the mob breaks its pledge and the fickle whore/falls back)

In this incomprehensible address to Fortune, there is contrast, as Nisbet and Hubbard see, between *rara* and *uolgus*, *Fides* and

infidum, nec comitem abnegat and *retro cedit. Fides* also makes a clear
counterpoise to *meretrix periura*. Since this is so, and since *Fides* is
draped in white, a strong invitation is issued to our visual imagination to see against the white of *Fides* the contrasting gaudiness
of the prostitute. Such is the characteristic difference between
married woman and *meretrix* (*Epistles*, 1.18.3–4):

> ut matrona meretrici dispar erit atque
> discolor.

A simile is an invitation to visualize resemblances (IV.2.25–32):

> *multa Dircaeum leuat* aura *cycnum,*
> tendit, Antoni, quotiens in *altos*
> *nubium* tractus: ego *apis Matinae*
> more modoque,
> grata carpentis *thyma per laborem*
> *plurimum*, circa nemus uuidique
> Tiburis *ripas operosa paruos*
> carmina fingo.

(Antonius, a great wind lifts the swan of Dirce/whenever it
soars into the lofty tracts/of the clouds: I am like a bee/
from the Matine hill/harvesting the lovely thyme with
enormous/labour. Along the dripping banks/of wooded
Tibur, in my own small way/I mould laborious songs.)

This is a 'dissimile', an invitation to visualize contrasts. The
breeze lifts the swan; Horace, like a bee, has no such extraneous
assistance (*per laborem plurimum, operosa*); Pindar is the swan of
Dirce, the famous fountain of Thebes which resounds through
Greek lyric poetry; Horace is the bee of a mountain or promon-
tory or plain (we still do not know what Matinum was and it is
not mentioned in extant poetry before Horace). In the first book of
the *Odes* also it appears in a belittling context (I.28.1–4):

> Te *maris et terrae numeroque carentis* harenae
> mensorem cohibent, *Archyta,*
> *pulueris exigui* prope litus *parua Matinum*
> munera.

(You have measured the sea, Archytas, the earth/and the
unnumbered sand. You are now confined/near the Matine
shore by the tiny tribute/of a little dust.)

The swan flies high *in altos nubium tractus*; the bee works the river bank, and thyme is a creeper. So much for bilateral contrasts; but the wealth of this poetry depends also upon unilateral contrasts, where only one member of the pair is mentioned. The swan is proverbial for the sweetness of its singing; we are left to imagine the buzzing of the bee. *Multa aura* is all very well for swans; but not for bees, as all readers of Virgil knew ('principio sedes apibus statioque petenda,/quo neque sit uentis aditus', *Georgics*, IV.8-9). The river bank and the trees are other requisites of bees which lend poetic strength to this metaphor and they too are stressed early in the fourth *Georgic* (18-24). So too *fingo* is a bee word (*Georgics*, IV.57 and 179). And the minuteness of the bees is a motif of Virgil's masterpiece, exploited by Horace as are all the other bee references noted in this stanza in a similar context in *Epistles*, 1.3.[21]

Contrast and metaphor

There are many passages in Horace where we can see the characteristic Horatian contrast if we see the literal force of the words (1.16.17-20):

> irae Thyesten exitio *graui*
> *strauere* et *altis* urbibus ultimae
> *stetere* causae, cur perirent
> *funditus inprimeretque* muris . . .

(Anger laid Thyestes low in a heavy doom,/and stands revealed as the primary reason/for the destruction of lofty cities to their foundations/and the razing of their walls . . .)

Nisbet and Hubbard comment upon *stetere*, 'anger is the appointed or determined cause', and they write that *altis* means 'great and proud' rather than 'high'. But there is more to it than that. Surely in this context *stetere* and *altis* are set against *graui*, *strauere* and *inprimeret*? This is not to argue for my translation 'standing' *rather* than 'appointed', for 'high' *rather* than 'proud'. The translation is offered to isolate the point. The words do mean what Nisbet and Hubbard say they mean. They have at the same time another function.

The contrasts are more elaborate, but they also lead to the literal force of the words in (II.4.9-12):

> barbarae postquam cecidere turmae
> *Thessalo uictore* et *ademptus Hector*
> tradidit *fessis leuiora tolli*
> *Pergama Grais.*

(After the barbarian squadrons fell/to the Thessalian
conqueror and the removal of Hector/made the taking of
Troy/a lighter task for the weary Greeks.)

The last line presents the standard contrast of nations at its
barest. The second line has a similar confrontation but with
variation in shape and content, the Thessalian victor and the
removed Hector. But more important for the poetry is the
relationship between *leuiora* and *tolli*. Of course this means that
Troy was easier to capture, but it presents the reader with an
extra picture. If the removal of Hector makes Troy *leuiora tolli*, we
are driven to see the literal sense of *ademptus*, and of *leuiora*, and of
tolli. Horace plays the same trick in III.4.44, '*immanemque turbam
fulmine* sustulerit caduco' – 'he destroyed (and caught *up*) the monstrous horde with his *falling* thunderbolt'.[22]
Sometimes contrast leads to the literal meaning of the word
and this exposes a pun (IV.11.25–8):

> terret ambustus Phaethon auaras
> spes et exemplum *graue* praebet *ales*
> *Pegasus terrenum equitem grauatus*
> *Bellerophontem,*

(The burning of Phaethon frightens our greedy hopes./
Winged Pegasus, throwing off the weight/of his earthly
rider Bellerophon, provides/a weighty example,)

'There is a half comic irony', observes Wickham in his commentary, 'in the array of mythological instances of the folly of
misplaced ambition.' There is also a pun, and carefully disposed
contrasts to lead us to it. *ales Pegasus terrenum equitem* is the usual
tooling and *grauatus Bellerophontem* completes the pattern: Pegasus
and Bellerophon; winged and earthly; the tossing of the rider. In
this setting when *Pegasus grauatus exemplum graue praebet*, the
example is weighty, not sharp. *graue grauatus* is not a slovenly
repeat, but a pointed polyptoton. There are two passages in
Lucretius which may have sparked off this pattern of thought:

41

one, his pun on *grauis* where downy seed-heads find it no light task to fall (*qui nimia leuitate cadunt plerumque grauatim*, III.387); two, where Lucretius is taking the credulous to task for their belief that lightning is the weapon of the gods, and asks in a cataract of rhetorical questions why they strike the innocent as well as the guilty (VI.390–2):

> cur quibus incautum scelus auersabile cumquest
> non faciunt icti flammas ut fulguris halent
> pectore perfixo, documen mortalibus acre?

(Why do they not so ordain that men guilty of loathsome crimes/should be struck by lightning and made to exhale its flames/through their riven breasts? That would be a sharp lesson for mortals.)

Sharp indeed, not to say acrid, since lightning burns with the smell of sulphur: (*grauis halantes sulpuris auras*, VI.221).

A clear example may now lead us to something more elusive (II.3.1–2):

> *aequam* memento rebus in *arduis*
> seruare mentem

(Try to stay level-headed when the going/is rough.)

The word *arduis* is used seven times in the *Odes*,[23] and always with its literal sense of 'steep', as in the triple contrast *arduis pronos relabi* (1.29). As the commentators see, opposition between *aequam* and *arduis* framing the first line of II.3 above, guarantees here too the presence of the literal force. This assists our understanding of 1.3:

> expertus uacuum Daedalus aera
> pinnis non homini datis;
> perrupit Acheronta Herculeus labor.
> nil mortalibus ardui est:
> caelum ipsum petimus stultitia neque
> per nostrum patimur scelus
> iracunda Iouem ponere fulmina. (1.3.34–40)

(Daedalus tried the empty air/with superhuman wings./The labour of Hercules/burst through the underworld. No path is too steep for mortals:/we scale the sky itself in our

foolishness/and by our sin we prevent Jupiter/from laying
aside his anger, and his lightning.)

Commentators sometimes condemn this ode without mentioning
the two main sources of poetic power at the end of it: one, the
allusion to the Civil Wars as a divine judgment on contemporary
Rome; two, the visualization. Three offences are listed: man's
first flight, the descent into the underworld, the scaling of
Olympus (*per arduum*, II.19.21). All of these offenders went by a
steep road, and *ardui* in its literal sense links them all and gives the
passage a sensory vitality. The word is often interpreted simply as
'difficult' and the line explained as a reflection of Greek commonplaces. This is half the story. The commonplaces cited have not
the serious topical relevance of Horace. Nor his visualization.

Our last cluster of contrasts and metaphors is a virtuoso piece
(III.28.1–8):

> Festos quid potius die
>> Neptuni faciam? *prome reconditum,*
> Lyde, *strenua* Caecubum
>> *munitaeque adhibe uim* sapientiae.
> *inclinare* meridiem
>> sentis et, ueluti *stet uolucris* dies,
> *parcis deripere* horreo
>> *cessantem Bibuli* consulis amphoram?

(What better is there for me to do/on Neptune's day? Up
with you, Lyde./Draw out the long-stored Caecuban/and
mount an attack on the citadel of wisdom./You see the
midday giving way, and yet/as though the flying day were
standing fast/do you spare the shirking jar of Bibulus the
consul,/and hesitate to tear it out from its cellar?)

Once again the oppositions force us to appreciate the metaphors.
Strenuitas is a cardinal military virtue, guaranteed by *munitae* and
adhibe uim. But if Lyde is asked *strenua* to bring out the *cessantem
amphoram*, the jar is not just delaying, it is shirking battle.[24] This
alerts us to *parcis* which must in such a context flick at its military
sense. And *cessantem* is opposed not only to *strenua* but also to
deripere. The jar is lingering, so it should be hustled out of the
cellar. *Cessantem* and *Bibuli* are in discord and at the same time in
harmony: in discord, because a man with the name of Bibulus

should be ready to tipple and therefore anything but hesitant; in harmony, because Bibulus was famous for his procrastination during the consulship of Julius Caesar.

There is another conspicuous contrast. Lyde sees the midday sun *departing* from the vertical, and yet she temporizes as though the fleeting day were *standing* still. *Inclinare* and *stet*, in this astronomical sense, are in polar tension. But we have seen a clearly marked military metaphor in ll. 3 and 4 and 7 and 8. *Inclinare* and *stare* in ll. 5 and 6 may also be playing with a military sense. *Inclinare* is a technical military term for the buckling of a line of battle (e.g. *inclinatur acies*, Livy, 1.12.3) and *stare* is its opposite. If this opposition is felt to be part of the military allusion, the logic of the metaphor is under strain. Who are the contestants in this battle? Lyde is attacking the barricades of wisdom. The *amphora* of wine is shirking and Lyde is 'sparing to drag it out', so it seems to be a potential ally. But already the metaphor is strained. Normally it is an enemy that would be spared, not an ally. And how are the forces of time aligned? There is no need to ask. The allusion may be an enlargement and complication rather than a precise analogy. Horace is playing with contrasts and images, not model-building.

Contrast and tone of voice

adduxere sitim tempora, Vergili.
sed *pressum* Calibus ducere *Liberum*
si gestis, iuuenum nobilium cliens,
    nardo uina merebere.
nardi paruus onyx eliciet cadum,
qui nunc Sulpiciis *accubat* horreis,
spes donare nouas largus amaraque
    curarum eluere efficax.
ad quae si *properas* gaudia, cum tua
uelox merce ueni: non ego te meis
inmunem meditor *tingere* poculis,
    plena diues ut in domo.
uerum pone *moras* et studium lucri . . .
               (IV.12.13–25)

(These are thirsty times Virgil, but if/you fancy a draught of vintage from the presses/of Cales, you client of the young

nobility,/you must pay for your wine with nard./A small box
of nard will tempt out the jar of wine/now reclining in the
cellars of Sulpicius./It will grant you new hopes in abundance/
and effectively wash away the bitterness of sorrow./If you
are in a hurry to taste these joys, come quickly/with your
barter: I do not intend to let you dip/in my cups scotfree, as
though I were/a rich man in a full house./But throw aside
delay and your eagerness for profit . . .)

This essay has freely hypothesized puns and word-play, but there
are limits. The last phrase of the first book, *arta sub uite bibentem*,
leaves Horace drinking under the dense foliage of a vine, not as
M. O. Lee[25] believes, thinking of *uita uiuentem*, not at all; and not
at all thinking that the phrase echoes *sera morietur*, which Lee
conjures out of *sera moretur* in the previous stanza. Nor should
Bacchus (*Liber*) leap to the mind as we read *nunc est bibendum nunc
pede libero* (1.37.1), as Commager proposes.[26] True the play on
these two meanings occurs in Plautus (*Captiui*, 577; *Cistellaria*, 127),
but *pede Libero* makes no sense. *Pressum ducere Liberum* (IV.12.14) is
slightly more tempting because of the standard polarity of the
expression, 'to lead free what had been pressed' (cf. *Satires*,
II.4.69, 'pressa *Venafranae quod baca* remisit *oliuae*').

A small box of nard is set against the abundant hopes, the onyx
box perhaps against the earthenware jar, the coaxing out against
the reclining in the cellars, freshness against bitterness, hopes
against cares, giving against washing away,[27] with goods as
opposed to empty-handed, haste as opposed to delay. Less
obvious is the interplay between the washing away and the dip-
ping, but not less characteristic. Wine effectively washes away
bitterness, but Virgil is not going to be allowed to dip in it.
Another possible crosscurrent is the interaction of *efficax* and
immunem after *Liberum*, both adjectives being used elsewhere by
Horace in religious contexts (*Epodes*, 3.17; 17.1; *Odes*, III.23.17).

Virgil has been dead for half-a-dozen years and here is Horace
calling him 'a client of the young nobility' and teasing him for his
desire to make money. 'If we find anything offensive in these
phrases as applied to the poet Virgil it is surely only because for us
Virgil is not, as he was for Horace, the friend with whom we have
joked and drunk wine on the road to Brindisi.' So argues L. A.
Moritz,[28] and explains the commercial references as a private joke

between the two. Perhaps a straw of support for this contention may be found in the only two other passages in the Odes where Horace mentions Virgil's name.

The first of these is addressed to the ship on which Virgil is sailing to Greece (1.3.5–8):

> nauis quae tibi *creditum*
> *debes* Virgilium: finibus Atticis
> *reddas* incolumem precor
> et serues animae dimidium meae.

(You are the ship to whom Virgil has been entrusted./You owe him. Pay him intact I beg you/to the land of Attica,/ and keep safe the half of my life.)

'One is meant to think', according to Nisbet and Hubbard, 'of a valuable object deposited with a friend for safe keeping.' Yes. But, in fact, *creditum, debes* and *reddas* could cover a wide range of commercial or financial transactions and *dimidium* suggests rather the deposit or loan of a sum of money.[29] The second reference is similar (1.24.9–12):

> multis ille bonis flebilis occidit,
> nulli flebilior quam tibi, Vergili.
> tu frustra pius, heu, non ita *creditum*
> *poscis* Quintilium deos.

(Now he is dead and many good men will weep for him,/but none more than you Virgil. You pray the gods/with useless devotion, to give back Quintilius./He was not entrusted to us on those terms.)

The three references to the name of Virgil in the *Odes* of Horace are all associated with commercial or financial allusions. Coincidence? Aided by the fact that these motifs occur in other *propemptica* and *consolationes*?[30] Perhaps. But 'Horace is the poet, above all, of human relationships', and commentators amply demonstrate his penchant for banter.[31] This is *ad hominem* poetry. Its allusions are often lost irretrievably. Its tone was for the ears of a small circle of friends. Virgil was Horace's friend, and generally thought to be the greatest of the Roman poets. Horace twice mentions his name in mercantile contexts, and now, so soon after his death, speaks of him as a mercenary social climber. It is just conceivable that this was some private joke between the two. It is not conceivable that the tone of IV.12 could be malicious. The coarseness directed towards Horace in the letters of Augustus preserved by Suetonius shows that this coterie enjoyed offensive endearments. The tone of this ode must be affectionate.

In this study of contrasts in the *Odes*, certain points of technique have been seen to recur. We shall gather these together by study-ing one whole poem (II.10):

> Rectius uiues, Licini, neque altum   1
> semper urgendo neque, dum procellas
> cautus horrescis, nimium premendo
>   litus iniquum.
> auream quisquis mediocritatem   5
> diligit, tutus caret obsoleti
> sordibus tecti, caret inuidenda
>   sobrius aula.
> saeuius uentis agitatur ingens   9
> pinus et celsae grauiore casu
> decidunt turres feriuntque summos
>   fulgura montis.
> sperat infestis, metuit secundis   13
> alteram sortem bene praeparatum
> pectus: informis hiemes reducit   15
>   Iuppiter, idem
> submovet; non, si male nunc, et olim   17
> sic erit: quondam cithara tacentem   18
> suscitat Musam neque semper arcum
>   tendit Apollo.
> rebus angustis animosus atque   21
> fortis adpare, sapienter idem
> contrahes uento nimium secundo
>   turgida uela.

(You will live better Licinius, if you don't always go straining over the high seas, nor should you worry about storms and hug the rocky coast too close.

47

Whoever loves the Golden Mean is safe,
without the squalor of a filthy garret,
and moderate, without a mansion
for men to envy.

The huge pine tree is tossed more violently
by winds, the high towers come down
with a heavier fall, the lightning strikes
the top of the mountains.

The well-prepared heart hopes in adversity
for a change in fortune, and fears in prosperity
a change in fortune.

Jupiter brings back
ugly winters and Jupiter
removes them.

If life is bad now, it won't
always be bad.

sometimes Apollo rouses
the silent Muse with his lyre. It's not always
his bow he stretches.

When things are tight show spirit
and courage. When the wind is too strong
at your back, be sensible, shorten
the bulging sail.)

The gaps in the translation show that this poem is a series of eight antitheses (ten if we count the third stanza as three). Each appears to express some aspect of the Golden Mean. This may therefore be viewed as a string of ten examples of the same rhetorical figure devoted to the same ethical commonplace. Unpromising raw material. How does Horace make poetry out of it?

First, the disposition of the antitheses. As the line numbers show, the first three stanzas are coextensive with the first three antitheses. Then the even divisions cease. The next three antitheses progressively decrease in length, each ending in the middle of a line, one of them striding over a stanza. The next increases again, and even division is restored in the last stanza, all forming a kind of ring composition. Counterpoint between sense and line and stanza is difficult to expound, but easy and live to hear, and part of the dramatic pacing of the poem.

Horace varies not only the length of the antitheses but also their shape. Lines 6–8 run ABCD BCAD, with BC representing the close responsion of *caret inuidenda* to *caret obsoleti* at the end of successive lines. In the third stanza huge trees are tossed more violently, tall towers fall more heavily, and lightning strikes the top of the mountains. In each colon the phrasing is varied, the word order is tellingly disposed in counterpoint to the line endings, and the opposites are left to our imagination. Line 13 is ABAB; ll. 15–17 ABBA; ll. 17–18, *non si male nunc et olim sic erit*, not if AB, BA, the starkest possible expression of the transitoriness of bad fortune; ll. 18–20 defy formulae, but none the less they present three pairs of interacting elements (sometimes, not always; the lyre and the bow; the rousing and the stretching, an irregular ABC ABC).

The manipulation of metaphor is vital to this poem. Ring composition is visible again, the relationship between the navigational metaphor in the first stanza and the nautical metaphor in the last. Within each of these the details are precise and active in the poem, like *semper* and *iniquum*. It would be foolhardy *always* to cut across the open sea. Equally it is dangerous to hug a coast too close if it is *rocky*. The full force of some of the metaphors is grasped only after we apprehend the contrasts round about them. *urgere altum* for instance, is an intensive variation of the normal phrase *tenere altum*, to steer across the high seas, suggesting *inter alia* the impatience of the sailor; but the force of *altum semper urgendo* depends upon its audible correspondence with *nimium premendo litus*. Similarly, it is the context which illumines the Golden Mean. This dazzling oxymoron has been too successful. We are too familiar with it to realize how provocative it is, and how it fits the argument. Mediocrity is drab. In calling it golden, Horace is differentiating it from the squalor of poverty (*obsoleti sordibus tecti*), and also from the rich man's palace (*inuidenda aula*).[32] It is the mean that is truly golden, not the golden gewgaws of the wealthy (cf. Lucretius, II.24–8). In the second last stanza, again the antithesis leads to a keener apprehension of the image. Apollo sometimes rouses the Muse with his lyre; he does not always stretch the bow. This invites us to visualize Apollo stretching the strings of the lyre. And finally, in the nautical metaphor, the contrasts again stimulate the senses. When things are tight (*rebus angustis*) you don't tighten your bulging sails (*contrahes turgida uela*); when the favouring wind is too strong (*uento nimium secundo*) you don't show yourself to be high-spirited (*animosus*). It is reasonable in reading this poet to be led by the carefully tooled contrast to think of the application of the word *animosus* to winds (*animosi Euri*, Virgil, *Georgics*, II.441).

The argument of the poem is well constructed. Aristotle's treatment of virtue as a mean provides a useful comparison. 'In the section confined to the feelings inspired by danger you will observe that the mean state is "courage". Of those who go to extremes in one direction or the other the man who shows an excess of fearlessness has no name to describe him, the man who exceeds in confidence or daring is called "rash" or "foolhardy", the man who shows an excess of fear and a deficiency of confidence is called a "coward".'[33] And so Aristotle moves systematically through the same sort of material as Horace from the mean of courage with an extreme on each side of it, to the mean as applied to the giving and acquiring of money, to ambition, to man's attitudes to the fortunes of neighbours. Horace's argument is less clearly signposted than Aristotle's, but no less valid and dynamic. The first three stanzas hang together. Always taking risks is one extreme and it is contrasted with a nervous excess of precautions. *iniquo* is anything but a vacuous epithet. Horace is making the interesting point that an excess of caution leads to danger. The next two stanzas apply the doctrine of the mean to wealth and to eminence. The fourth stanza propounds a new but related thesis, that the man whose mind is well-prepared is ready for a reversal of fortune. This reversability of fortune is then asserted three times, beginning with Jupiter, then in the barest possible terms which cannot but speak directly to Licinius' predicament ('non si male nunc et olim/sic erit'), then with reference to Apollo. The final stanza pulls together the two topics of the mean of courage and the reversability of fortune, and relates them: when Fortune is adverse, be brave; be cautious when she is favourable. This ode is not a repetitive string of clichés. The final thesis has not previously been propounded. It is the conclusion of the argument. Characteristic of the Pindaric style of Horace are the 'abrupt admonitions' and 'portentous maxims paratactically introduced.' But the absence of connectives does not mean the absence of connection. Equally characteristic of Horace are the shaping and movement of the argument. This is an intelligent rumination on two generalizations culminating in a combination of them.

Williams[34] suggests that much of the life and tension of moralizing poetry depends upon the movement from particular to general. In this poem this movement is vividly manifested in the syntax. The first stanza is addressed to Licinius and his name appears in the vocative with a verb in the second person jussive future. The poem then moves from the personal to the universal with *quisquis* in l. 5, and gives a series of generalizations mounting to Jupiter and Apollo. In the last stanza it returns to the second person with an imperative and another jussive future, completing yet another ring composition.

And the personal element is vital. This is *ad hominem* poetry, and expounded as such by Hanslik.[35] Aulus Terentius Varro Murena (formerly Licinius Murena) was consul in 23 B.C. He was removed from office by Augustus in the summer of 23. This ode was then written. In the next year he defended M. Primus on a charge of *maiestas*, joined the conspiracy of Fannius Caepio and was executed. 'Every word in Horace's Ode corresponds to the situation,' writes Hanslik. 'The cares of his friend were his own and he was trying not only to please Murena but also to improve him and help him.' This claim appears to be near the truth. The third stanza, for instance, is less abstract than it appears to be. If it was written immediately after Murena's removal from office, it takes on a tone at once complimentary and consolatory. 'You reached the pinnacle of political ambition. You must not be surprised if you were in an exposed position.' The first stanza is also topical, striking a judicious balance between foolhardiness and over-caution; the last (and the difference is useful and thoughtful) strikes the balance between courage and over-confidence. In electing to defend Primus, Murena missed both of these golden means.

But Hanslik claims too much. After three articles in *Historia*[36] in recent years it is still not possible to be certain of the precise dating of Murena's career and therefore of the precise application of the words of Horace's ode. Equally it may be an over-simplification to talk of 'advice'. Sometimes he gives the impression that he is advising the great to do what he knows they have already decided to do. This is eulogy rather than admiration. But the essential point stands. The poem has a purchase in real life. It spoke thoughtfully and directly to a man who had to contend with a problem which was to bring him to his death. This we should allow for, as we read the apparently abstract moralizing. 'Horace is the poet, above all, of human relationships.'

Appendix 1 *Sustained images*

When a *single* word is used in Latin in a metaphorical sense it is difficult to be sure whether its literal sense is felt. It would be rash to insist upon any notion of flowering or heat in *adhuc florente iuuenta feruidus*, still hot in the flower of youth (*Ars Poetica*, 115–16); and foolish to think of fertility when Mercury delivers the souls of the dead to their joyous abodes (*tu pias laetis animas reponis sedibus, Odes*, 1.10.17), or of nursing when time snatches along the kindly day (*almum quae rapit hora diem*, IV.7.7).

When *two* or *more* words appear to be involved in the metaphor it is safer initially to assume that the metaphor is alive. The notion of nursing is not absent from *alit* alongside *nutrix* (1.22.14–16); *feruens* with *tumet* (1.13.4) suggests boiling; *laetas florere* in Lucretius (1.255) suggests that identity of human and vegetable growth which is fundamental to the argument of the whole passage.

But even with two or more terms there is room for doubt. Sometimes the literal sense of the words does not fit closely enough. *generat* for instance between *alit* and *nutrix* just cited (1.22) confuses the functions of the sexes. Similarly *rectius* in the navigational metaphor at the beginning of II.10 could well in theory introduce the notion of a straight course but that does not fit the navigational context. Sometimes the literal sense is not frequently enough attested. This may tell against any literal force in *animosus* (II.10.21). Sometimes the metaphor itself is ill suited. The argument requires 'spirited' at that point, not 'windy'. Sometimes coincidence or mechanical word association may have brought together words which do not work together. So perhaps *inclinare* and *stare* (III.28) and *pressum Liberum* (IV.12) noted above.

There *is* an area for disagreement. But scepticism has gone too far. Some views are just wrong. To question the vegetative image in *laetas florere* (Lucretius, 1.255) because Cicero frequently uses *florere* without any reference to flowers; or to question another image because if it were felt, it would end in the middle of a sentence; or to question the application of a simile to the surrounding argument because the simile is comprehensible without recourse to that argument—this is bad method.[37] Nisbet and Hubbard are also cautious, but at a different level, in their general assessment of Horace. 'By and large he avoids alliteration, onomatopoeia, and haunting vowel sounds: he does not evoke more than he says. His metaphors are sparse and trite.'[38] The first colon of the assessment could be refuted by reference to almost anything that L. P. Wilkinson has written on Horace, and to any reader whose ear has ever been haunted by a phrase from the *Odes*. The rest of it is annulled by the alert apprehension of allusions and images in their own great commentary, for example the legal flavour of *fruitur credulus aurea qui semper vacuam* (1.5) and the shepherding in *compulerit Mercurius gregi* after *uirga* (1.24). Their extremity of caution (*nimium premendo litus iniquum*) is perhaps to be explained as an over-reaction to some of the work on imagery being done at the moment in the United States (*altum semper urgendo*). It is not easy to remain temperate on reading for example that in the third stanza of 11.10 '*celsae* implies the expansiveness of life; *graviore* the confining oppression of death',[39] or that in 1.5 Pyrrha is 'like a Siren on a Siren's rock' and also 'like the living-dead golden bough' and also 'akin to the *nitentes Cycladas*', and on the next page that she 'becomes a beacon fire that lures ignorant seafarers to their destruction' and also 'the pyre on which they suffer the *ardor* not of love but of death'.[40] These promiscuous associations do not touch the poem. But they sully the critic. It is worse than useless to posit a meaningful interaction between words in widely separate contexts in obvious defiance of the apprehension of any normal reader or listener, and of the obvious statistics of language. When a word or image recurs in a Latin poet, we do not always have to believe that he is passing an arcane comment upon its occurrence 500 lines before.

Horace is not a brilliant excogitator of new similitudes. In his imagery he often falls short of the euphony and passion of Virgil. But in other respects he is superior. He lifts the old metaphor up to the light and turns it round and sees new facets and colours in it and relates these in new ways to each other and to the reality he is trying to illustrate, always with a wide range of subtly differentiated emotional tone, often with humour. It is enough to compare

And it is no accident that *four*-year-old wine is kept in a *two*-eared jar.

The third relevant fact of Horace's language is his tendency to achieve weird effects by juxtaposing parts of the body. Once again Virgil provides examples of similar technique put to different work, for example when Palinurus clutched with his hands at the heads of the mountain ('prensantemque uncis *manibus capita* aspera montis', *Aeneid*, VI.360). Similarly in the account of the wounds of love sustained by Dido, we read that there was sticking in her, piercing her breast – and expect the subject to be some weapon – it is a face: 'Haerent infixi *pectore uoltus*/uerbaque' (*Aeneid*, IV.4–5).

Horace shows that he realizes that this trick can misfire by beginning his *Ars Poetica* by making fun of painters who depict animals with human heads and horses' necks, and other such Chimaeras dire ('humano *capiti ceruicem* pictor equinam iungere si uelit . . .'). When he writes about Orpheus drawing with his lute the eared oak trees (*auritas ducere quercus*, I.12.11–12), he is flamboyantly courting a similar disaster. This is not pomposity or ineptitude, but a humorous delight in mythology taken to its logical conclusion, and he often evinces this delight. So with the conjunction of foot and thumb in IV.6.35–6 where *pedem* means a metrical foot. So when the crowd in the underworld is packed shoulder to shoulder drinking in with their ears (*densum umeris bibit aure uolgus*, II.13.32). Here the quasi-chiastic structure alerts the mind to the relationship between the parts so symmetrically ordered. To mould this symmetry the strange expression, *densum umeris*, dense with the shoulders, is excogitated to balance *aure uolgus*. Further, in a language as sensitive as Latin to the literal sense of words, to drink with the ear is something of a feat. And why many shoulders, but a single ear? The answer is at one level metrical, at another it is an intellectual provocation.

Horace is enjoying the same kind of nonsense in (II.19.1–4):

> Bacchum in remotis carmina rupibus
> uidi docentem, credite posteri,
> Nymphasque discentis et auris
> capripedum Satyrorum acutas.

(I have seen, believe me all you generations to come,/
Bacchus teaching among the remote crags/and the Nymphs

learning and the ears/of the goatfooted Satyrs cocked to listen.)

Bacchus is teaching, the Nymphs learning, so when we are told that the ears of the Satyrs are sharp, the formal antithesis forces us to realize that the sharpness is not just an anatomical description. [41] So much is unmistakable. But within this conceit about the Satyrs there is embedded a contrast, *auras capripedum*, 'the ears of the goatfooted.' The result of this jugglery is to heighten the weird and wonderful effect of the scene. This harmonizes with the plea, *credite posteri*, 'believe me, future generations,' which, according to Williams, [42] 'strikes a note which is characteristic of the style of rather lighthearted, cynical, Hellenistic poetry'. Juxtaposition of different parts of the body is combined with a numerical play in (II.13.33–5):

> quid mirum, ubi illis carminibus stupens
> demittit atras belua centiceps
>   auris . . .

(Little wonder when the hundred-headed beast/is struck dumb by these songs and its ears/drop . . .)

All two hundred of them we calculate, seeing the characteristic collocation, *centiceps auris*. There is another example of anatomical number play when Cerberus licks the feet and legs of Bacchus with his triple-tongued mouth (II.19.31–2):

> recedentis trilingui
> ore pedes tetigitque crura

After we disentangle the anatomy and the language which expresses it, we may, with Horace, lose sight of common sense and be ready to entertain the possibility that in *quadrimum Sabina merum diota* we are to savour a triple conceit, the Sabine against the Greek, the four against the two, and the numeration of the ears. [43]

If so, we should catch a similar conceit flickering in *sustulerit caduco*, and in many other examples of surrealism and παρὰ προσδοκίαν in this strange poet. In *Ars Poetica*, 47–8 Horace argues that poetic excellence is a matter of making the old word new by placing it in a cunning setting. The very form of this utterance from *notum* to *nouum*, AB AC BA ('notum *si callida uerbum/reddiderit iunctura* nouum') gives a hint that whatever else *callida iunctura* means, it includes this sort of word order. And if this kind of placing makes words new, it sometimes does so by interactions like those posited in this chapter.

Notes

1 G. Williams, *Tradition and Originality in Roman Poetry*, Oxford, 1968; *The Third Book of Horace's Odes*, Oxford, 1969.

2 R. G. M. Nisbet and M. Hubbard, *A Commentary on Horace Odes Book I*, Oxford, 1970.

3 E. Norden, *P Vergilius Maro Aeneis Buch VI*, Darmstadt, 1957 on line 321.

4 N. E. Collinge, *The Structure of Horace's Odes*, London, 1961. The quotation is from p. 36. Further examples are given by E. Stemplinger, *RE*, 8 (1912), 2384 s.v. 'Horatius'. See also F. Bücheler, Index Scholarum Hib. Bonnae, 1878–9; *Kleine Schriften*, Leipzig and Berlin, 1915–30, 2.318–19, 'huiusmodi oxymora cum multis Romanis placuerunt tum maxime Horatio cui fatendum erit grammatici quam poetici ingenii benigniorem fuisse venam.'

5 M. Schuster, *RE*, 2.7 (1948) 2388 s.v. 'Valerius'.

6 E. Fraenkel, *Horace*, Oxford, 1957, 239.

7 These contrasts confirm the comma after *procax* and not before it. She is *procax*, immoral, as opposed to *severae*; not *procax* in the sense of exceeding her proper function by writing dirges. For more general studies of such poems see H. J. Mette, *Museum Helveticum*, 18 (1961), 136–9; and P. L. Smith, *AJP*, 89 (1968), 56–65.

8 R. G. M. Nisbet, *Critical Essays on Roman Literature: Elegy and Lyric*, ed., J. P. Sullivan, London, 1962, 192.

9 Williams, *Tradition*, 114.

10 See *Lucan*, I, ed. R. J. Getty, Cambridge, 1940, lv.

11 *Compescere* is used spatially with *fluentis ramos* (Virgil, *Georgics*, II. 370) and *spatianta bracchia* (Ovid, *Metamorphoses*, XIV, 630).

12 For other etymological plays see *superbos* pointed by *imo*, 1.35, and by *occidit*, IV.4.701 *Glycera* by *immitis*, 1.33; *Lyaeo* by *retegis*, III.21 and *solvere*, *Epode* IX.38; *duram* by *callet*, IV.9.49. For studies of II.14 see N. Rudd, *AJP*, 81 (1960), 376–9 and A. J. Woodman, *Latomus*, 26 (1967), 377–400. For other analyses which bring out contrasts in Horatian odes see H. Womble, *TAPA*, 92 (1961), 537–49 and S. Commager, *The Odes of Horace*, New Haven and London, 1962, 79–85.

13 Collinge, op. cit., 87–8.

14 These three heights are taken from H. Nissen, *Italische Landeskunde*, Berlin, 1902, 2, 908, 907 and 831.

15 See J. Henry, *Aeneidea*, Dublin, 1873–89, on *ingens* in *Aeneid* v.118.

16 *The Third Book of Horace's Odes*, 20 and Williams, *Tradition*, 600.

17 Fraenkel, op. cit., 229.

18 Williams, *Tradition*, 600.

19 On triremes see M. J. McGann, *Studies in Horace's First Book of Epistles*, Brussels, 1969, 22.

20 For other such contrasts see IV.2.23, 4.39–40, 7.21–5.

21 *Paruos* is in irrational tension with *multa*. The minuteness of bees and its implications are examined by Fraenkel, 437, and the other bee references by D. West, *Reading Horace*, Edinburgh, 1967, 30–9.

22 For a developed metaphor from the balance see *Satires*, 1.3.70–2. On *sustulerit caduco* see Appendix 1 and the pun on *tolli* at Velleius, 2.62.6.

23 1.3.37, 29.10; II.3.1, 19.21; III.4.21, 24.44, 29.10.

24 For the antithesis see 'quodsi cessas aut strenuos anteis', *Epistles*, 1.2.70; for the military force of *cessare* see 'cessantis ad arma concitet', *Odes* 1.35, and compare Cicero, *De Senectute*, 18.

25 M. O. Lee, *AJP*, 86 (1965), 280.

26 Commager, op. cit., 91.

27 For *amara* in a liquid metaphor cf. II.16.26. For *eluere* of washing out a dye see Lucretius 6.1077.

28 L. A. Moritz, *GR*, 16 (1969), 174–6, 187–93, and *CQ*, 18 (1968), 119.

29 For *incolumis* of a sum of money see Plautus, *Persa*, 324, and compare Livy, VI.15.5.

30 On life as a loan see Pseudo-Plato, *Axiochus* 367B, and H. A. Khan, *Latomus* 26 (1967), 112–14.

31 For one example of banter see Nisbet and Hubbard on 1.29. The quotation is from Williams, *Tradition*, 83.

32 C. J. Reagan, *RSC*, 18 (1970), 182.

33 Aristotle, *Nichomachean Ethics*, 2.7, ed. J. A. K. Thomson.

34 Williams, *Tradition*, ch. 9.

35 R. Hanslik, *Rh. Mus*, 96 (1953), 282–7.

36 See Nisbet and Hubbard, op. cit., xxxvii, and *Oxford Classical Dictionary* (1970)² 1108.

37 M. L. Clarke, *CR*, 21 (1971), 41–3.

38 Nisbet and Hubbard, op. cit., xxii.

39 Reagan, op. cit., 183.

40 M. C. J. Putnam, *CP*, 65 (1970), 252–3.

41 'et ad audiendum et ad ipsarum aurium figuram' Pseudoacron ad loc.

42 Williams, *Tradition*, 69.

43 Compare K. J. Reckford, *Hermes*, 90 (1962), 476–83.

III

The Three Worlds of Horace's Satires

M. J. McGann

It has in recent years become widely recognized that much of Latin poetry sets before the reader a domain of the imagination where elements of a real Roman world are fused with material that is unmistakably Greek. In certain poems of Catullus, in the *Eclogues* of Virgil and in many of the *Odes* of Horace, the poet has created a world whose customs, institutions and material culture belong to no single social group firmly located in space or time. By bringing such amalgams into being he enables his audience to enter a realm which is other than everyday, a world of heightened perception and emotion –

> Là, tout n'est qu'ordre et beauté,
> Luxe, calme et volupté.

Satire, however, conveys little of this sense of otherness. In spite of an obvious debt to Greek popular philosophy, it is the most Roman of Latin poetic genres. Even when Horace makes 'rich Asia' the setting of a satire (1.7), the poem draws no sustenance from the fact unless it be when, for a moment, it echoes the panegyrics which Greeks and Orientals had long been accustomed to address to their princes and which they now offered to their Roman masters (23–5):[1]

> laudat Brutum, laudatque cohortem,
> solem Asiae Brutum appellat stellasque salubris
> appellat comites excepto Rege.

(He praises Brutus, and he praises his staff. Brutus he calls Asia's sun, and his companions, with the exception of Rex, he calls healthful planets.)

Neither the Roman empire nor even the Roman state is of much
concern to Horace in the *Satires*. His chief interest is the individual
and his relations with society. Out of his vision of the world
about him, though not exclusively out of this, the poet has created
the setting in which he treats this theme. This setting I shall call
'the world of self and society'. It has two aspects. First, there is
an area of mundane existence, peopled by lawyers and litigants,
bargees and philosophers, praetors, petty officials and poets. It
embraces the streets and great houses of Rome and the roads, inns
and small towns of Italy. Secondly, there is a private realm, where
the poet, alone or with his friends, finds a contentment which is
elsewhere denied him. This favoured domain is not so much an
area distinct from the mundane as the mundane itself visited by a
spirit of delight. That at least is the position in Book I, where the
poet may inhabit this domain when in his house at Rome or
walking the city streets or travelling the roads of Italy. In Book II,
however, the sixth satire suggests that this domain of delight
has taken physical shape as his newly acquired Sabine farm,
outside which contentment is hardly to be found. Society of
course contains folly and wickedness as well as friendship and
wisdom, but its calumniators and social climbers represent
deviations from a norm. The world of self and society is basically
a place of sanity.

But there were times when Horace had a very different vision.
Like other satirists, he was capable of seeing in the world a
domain of madness in which men are enslaved to vice. He
refrained, however, from directly committing himself in either
of the two satires which most clearly spring from a vision of this
kind (II.3 and II.7), preferring instead to allow speakers of dubious
authority to make the running and appearing himself in the poems
as a character who undermines their pretensions. Yet in the end
their picture of a world insane and enslaved to passion remains
an integral and serious part of the whole satiric vision embodied
in the two books.

Lastly, there is the world of art, in which the poet's activity
is turned upon itself so that the domain within which the worlds
of self and society and of madness are realized is itself offered to
our contemplation.

Self and society

Satire is an urban genre, and for not a few satirists the great city has been a place of confusion, disorder and fear. Although something of this can be found in 11.6, it would be wrong to think of Rome in Horace's *Satires* as being in general either terrifying or grotesque. In the first book the poet appears to be perfectly at home there, blending solitude and society in a life of perfect contentment. As a boy he had been used to walk the streets of Rome with more ostentation than was appropriate in a freedman's son (1.6.78–82):

> vestem servosque sequentis,
> in magno ut populo, siqui vidisset, avita
> ex re praeberi sumptus mihi crederet illos.
> ipse mihi custos incorruptissimus omnes
> circum doctores aderat.

(Anyone who saw my clothes and attendant slaves, such as were called for in the midst of great crowds, would have believed that their cost was being met from an ancestral fortune. And my father himself was there, most incorruptible of guardians as I made the round of all the teachers.)

But as a civil servant, friend of Maecenas and poet with a name still to make, he walks with less display (1.6.111–14):

> quacumque libido est,
> incedo solus, percontor quanti holus ac far,
> fallacem circum vespertinumque pererro
> saepe forum, adsisto divinis.

(I go by myself wherever I fancy and ask the price of vegetables and meal. Often I wander through the Circus Maximus with its tricksters and the Forum at evening, and I stand beside the fortune-tellers.)

The most urban of the satires, 1.9, begins with the poet taking such a stroll, though this time he is accompanied by a slave (l. 10):

> Ibam forte via sacra, sicut meus est mos,
> nescio quid meditans nugarum, totus in illis:
> accurrit quidam notus mihi nomine tantum

(I happened to be going along the Sacra Via, thinking in
my usual way about some trifle or other and completely
absorbed in it, when up runs a fellow I know only by
name . . .) (1–3)

Although the action of the satire takes place entirely in the
streets of Rome, it imparts little of the flavour of a great, busy
metropolis. The poet's persistent companion, it is true, 'chatters
of anything, praising the streets and the town' (12–13), but of
traffic, shops or building activity there is not a word. The only
intrusion of the world of affairs arises from the fact that his
companion has to make an appearance in court (35–9):

> ventum erat ad Vestae, quarta iam parte diei
> praeterita, et casu tum respondere vadato
> debebat, quod ni fecisset, perdere litem.
> 'si me amas,' inquit 'paulum hic ades.' 'inteream, si
> aut valeo stare aut novi civilia iura.'

(With a quarter of the day already gone, Vesta's temple had
been reached, and it chanced that at that time he was obliged
to answer bail, and if he failed to, he would lose his case.
'Have a heart', said he, 'and give me a little support here'.
'I'm damned', said I, 'if I'm able to appear or if I know
anything about the law'.)

In the end it is this law-suit and the poet's readiness, in spite
of his claim to be ignorant of the law, to play his part in the
prescribed fashion which lead to his salvation (74–8):

> casu venit obvius illi
> adversarius et 'quo tu, turpissime?' magna
> inclamat voce, et 'licet antestari?' ego vero
> oppono auriculam, rapit in ius; clamor utrimque,
> undique concursus.

(The plaintiff chanced to meet him, and with a great shout
he called 'Where are you off to, you villain?' To me he said,
'May I have you as witness?' I offered him my ear. He
snatched him away to court, both of them shouting while the
people rushed from all around.)

Only at this point, with the reference to people running from all
directions (*undique concursus*), is the reader reminded that the

walk has taken place through a busy city. The poet has mentioned the Sacra Via, Caesar's park and the temple of Vesta, and
this imparts a certain, not altogether precise, sense of place to the
narrative. But Horace's concern is to describe a personal encounter, and to obtrude persons other than those directly involved, to mention beggar, philosopher or soldier would be to
distract from that concern. So Horace and his companion walk
through Rome insulated for most of the time from the busy life
about them.

The poet who in 1.6 and 1.9 strolled contentedly through
the Forum and Circus and along the Sacra Via was scarcely a
celebrity and attracted no public notice as he walked about. A
very different picture emerges from II.6. After he has appeared
as guarantor for a friend and taken on responsibilities which he
may later regret, he becomes the target of hostile comment as he
hurries to join Maecenas (28–31):

> luctandum in turba et facienda iniuria tardis.
> 'quid tibi vis, insane?' et 'quam rem agis?' inprobus urget
> iratis precibus, 'tu pulses omne quod obstat,
> ad Maecenatem memori si mente recurras?'

> (I am forced to struggle through the crowd, hurting those
> who are not quick enough. 'What do you mean, you
> madman?' and 'What are you up to?' demands a stubborn
> type with angry curses. 'So you think you can push
> everything that gets in your way if you are hurrying back to
> Maecenas and thinking only of him?')

At Maecenas' door there are messages awaiting him—a friend
expects his support in court tomorrow, his fellow civil servants
are holding an important meeting today and want him to attend.
A suitor in person asks him to see that Maecenas puts his seal on
a document and refuses to be satisfied with a promise to try.
Later a chilling rumour spreads through the streets (51–8):

> quicumque obvius est, me consulit: 'o bone – nam te
> scire, deos quoniam propius contingis, oportet –,
> numquid de Dacis audisti?' 'nil equidem.' 'ut tu
> semper eris derisor.' 'at omnes di exagitent me,

si quicquam.' 'quid? militibus promissa Triquetra
praedia Caesar an est Itala tellure daturus?'
iurantem me scire nihil mirantur ut unum
scilicet egregii mortalem altique silenti.

(I am consulted by everyone I meet: 'My dear fellow –
you're bound to know since it's your fate to be near
the top people – have you heard anything about the
Dacians?' 'Not a thing'. 'Just like you, always having a
laugh at our expense.' 'But I'm damned if I know anything.'
'Well then, what about the land Caesar promised the troops?
Is it going to be in Sicily or Italy?' When I swear I know
nothing, they regard me with amazement as a man without
equal for saying nothing.)

These are tiresome aspects of city life, but there is also a darker
side. At ll. 18–19 the poet speaks of the danger to health of
autumn in the city, and at the end of the satire the insignificance
and vulnerability of the individual in the city are hinted at through
the medium of fable. The country mouse is taking his ease with
his friend the town mouse in a great city mansion (111–17):

> 'cum subito ingens
> valvarum strepitus lectis excussit utrumque.
> currere per totum pavidi conclave magisque
> exanimes trepidare, simul domus alta Molossis
> personuit canibus. tum rusticus: "haud mihi vita
> est opus hac" ait et "valeas: me silva cavusque
> tutus ab insidiis tenui solabitur ervo." '

('when suddenly a great rattling of doors drove each from
his couch. In panic they ran the length of the dining room
and still more frightened were they when the tall house
echoed to the barking of Molossian hounds. Then said the
country mouse, "I've no need for this life. Goodbye. My
wood and mousehole safe from attack will keep me happy on
a plain diet".')

The personal indifference to matters of state suggested in ii.6
chimes well with the generally apolitical nature of the *Satires*
if not with some of the iambic poems upon which Horace was
working at about the same time. In i.6 the poet considers the
dignitas conferred on a candidate for office by the antiquity of his

family (9–44), and includes a succinct statement of the responsibilities which the candidate offers to undertake (34–5). But of the
realities of political life, the power of the armies and their generals
and the role of violence and corruption, he says nothing. In 1.5,
'The Journey to Brundisium', he only hints at the political
situation which forms the background to the journey: Maecenas
and Cocceius were 'each sent as delegates on matters of great
importance, being used to reconciling estranged friends' (28–9),
and Fonteius Capito was a loyal supporter of Antony (33). The
poet's concern is rather with offering a picture of life among the
travellers. What he chooses to say, however, is very much a
matter of externals, and the picture is by no means a revelation of
intimate details (31–2; 37–44; 48–9):

> interea Maecenas advenit atque
> Cocceius Capitoque simul Fonteius . . .
> in Mamurrarum lassi deinde urbe manemus,
> Murena praebente domum, Capitone culinam.
> postera lux oritur multo gratissima; namque
> Plotius et Varius Sinuessae Vergiliusque
> occurrunt, animae, qualis neque candidiores
> terra tulit neque quis me sit devinctior alter.
> o qui conplexus et gaudia quanta fuerunt.
> nil ego contulerim iucundo sanus amico . . .
> lusum it Maecenas, dormitum ego Vergiliusque;
> namque pila lippis inimicum et ludere crudis.

(Meanwhile Maecenas and Cocceius arrive together with
Fonteius Capito. . . . Then tired out we stay in the
city of the Mamurrae, Murena providing a house and Capito
a kitchen. By far the most welcome is the dawning of next
day, for in Sinuessa we are joined by Plotius, Varius and
Virgil – earth has not borne souls more honest, nor is any
other man closer to me. How we embraced and what joy
was ours! As long as I am in my senses, I would compare
nothing to a congenial friend . . . (In Capua) Maecenas goes
to play ball, Virgil and I to sleep, for the game is bad for
people with sore eyes or a poor digestion.)

'Sore eyes or a poor digestion': physical details are offered, and
there are more to come (84–5), but concerning what the friends

talked about, their views on books, politics or love, he preserves a silence, no less *egregium* and *altum* than that which met his questioners at 11.6.58.

The most vivid and genuinely amusing episode comes at the beginning, before Horace and Heliodorus are joined by the rest of the party (9–23):

> iam nox inducere terris
> umbras et caelo diffundere signa parabat:
> tum pueri nautis, pueris convicia nautae
> ingerere: 'huc adpelle'; 'trecentos inseris'; 'ohe,
> iam satis est.' dum aes exigitur, dum mula ligatur,
> tota abit hora. mali culices ranaeque palustres
> avertunt somnos; absentem cantat amicam
> multa prolutus vappa nauta atque viator
> certatim; tandem fessus dormire viator
> incipit ac missae pastum retinacula mulae
> nauta piger saxo religat stertitque supinus.
> iamque dies aderat, nil cum procedere lintrem
> sentimus, donec cerebrosus prosilit unus
> ac mulae nautaeque caput lumbosque saligno
> fuste dolat: quarta vix demum exponimur hora.

(Already was night preparing to draw shadows over the earth and scatter constellations upon the heavens when the slaves started hurling abuse at the bargees and the bargees at the slaves: 'Bring her along here', 'You're putting an army aboard', 'Steady on, that's enough'. While they ask for the fare and harness the mule, a whole hour passes. The frogs in the marshes and the accursed mosquitoes drive sleep away, and a bargee, well soused in flat wine, and one of the passengers have a competition in singing of the girls they left behind them. At length the passenger wearily falls asleep, and the lazy bargee turns the mule out to graze, ties the tow-rope to a rock and snores on his back. Day was already at hand when we realized that the boat wasn't moving. Then up started a hot-headed fellow who beat bargee and mule about the head and loins with a willow club. We scarcely made our point of disembarkation by 10 a.m.)

There is a pleasing detachment about this passage which contrasts with later episodes where the whole party seems united in being amused at the expense of certain ridiculous personages whose posturings feed the sophisticated travellers' sense of their own superiority (34–6):

> Fundos Aufidio Lusco praetore libenter
> linquimus, insani ridentes praemia scribae,
> praetextam et latum clavum prunaeque vatillum.

(We are glad to leave Fundi in the praetorship of the crazy scribe Aufidius Luscus, laughing at his insignia, the official toga and tunic and his ritual pan of live coals.)

During dinner they listen to a slanging match which begins when Sarmentus, a member of the party with a rather dubious background,[2] comments on the facial deformity of one of the local people present. They 'prolong that meal with absolute delight' (70). Their attentive host at Beneventum makes himself ridiculous by nearly burning down his house while preparing their meal (71–6), and at Gnatia the travellers laugh at local claims that in a temple there incense miraculously melts without fire (97–100). The impression of amused superiority which so much of the satire gives is not endearing.

A later poem, II.8, paints a picture that is no more attractive. Here Fundanius, who as a writer of comedies has an eye for the ridiculous, tells the poet how the rich Nasidienus entertained some guests, Maecenas and Varius among them, to a pretentious meal. When some hangings fall down raising clouds of dust, the host weeps bitterly and is comforted only after a sententious speech by one of his dependants about Fortune's cruelty. Varius, however, dear friend of Horace and Virgil and an *anima candidissima* (1.5.41–2), is scarcely able to hide a smirk (63–4). When Balatro, one of Maecenas' hangers-on, pays ironic tribute to the pains taken by the host (64–74), Nasidienus fails to see the irony and offers him fulsome thanks. When he goes on to serve still more delicacies and hold forth about them, the company takes vengeance by running away and leaving the dishes untasted. Nasidienus is of course a fool, but the sneering sense of superiority displayed by his guests goes far to redeem his pretentiousness.

But within the circle of Maecenas' friends there is no place for such an attitude at the expense of a fellow-member. On the contrary among friends, as the poet shows in 1.3, a man's vice should be reckoned a virtue (49–54):

> parcius hic vivit: frugi dicatur; ineptus
> et iactantior hic paulo est: concinnus amicis
> postulat ut videatur; at est truculentior atque
> plus aequo liber: simplex fortisque habeatur;
> caldior est: acris inter numeretur. opinor,
> haec res et iungit iunctos et servat amicos.

(One man lives in too sparing a fashion; let him be called temperate. Another is tactless and rather given to putting himself forward; he is simply asking to be thought agreeable by his friends. But another is quite aggressive and more free-spoken than is right; let him be regarded as frank and vigorous. Another is rather hot-tempered; let him be counted among men of spirit. This kind of response both binds men together and keeps them bound.)

But society in general is characterized by precisely the opposite kind of behaviour: virtues are 'turned upside down' (55–66):

> probus quis
> nobiscum vivit, multum demissus homo: illi
> tardo cognomen, pingui damus. hic fugit omnis
> insidias nullique malo latus obdit apertum,
> cum genus hoc inter vitae versemur, ubi acris
> invidia atque vigent ubi crimina: pro bene sano
> ac non incauto fictum astutumque vocamus.
> simplicior quis et est, qualem me saepe libenter
> obtulerim tibi, Maecenas, ut forte legentem
> aut tacitum inpellat quovis sermone: 'molestus,
> communi sensu plane caret' inquimus.

(An honest man lives among us, a very retiring fellow; we give him the name of slow and dull. Another avoids every pitfall, and since we live in this kind of world, where envy is biting and accusations flourish, he never leaves his flank open to an attack; instead of calling him sensible and cautious we say that he is false and too clever by half. Another is rather open, in the manner in which it has often been my fancy to present myself to you, Maecenas – when

his friend is reading or silent, he is liable to break in upon
him with any kind of remark; 'He's a pest', we say, 'and
completely without common tact'.)

In 1.4, where he is engaged in underlining the difference between
his own practice as a satirist and the malice of the backbiter, the
poet further illuminates the abrasiveness of Roman society (81–91;
93–100):

> absentem qui rodit, amicum
> qui non defendit alio culpante, solutos
> qui captat risus hominum famamque dicacis,
> fingere qui non visa potest, conmissa tacere
> qui nequit: hic niger est, hunc tu, Romane, caveto.
> saepe tribus lectis videas cenare quaternos,
> e quibus unus amet quavis aspergere cunctos
> praeter eum qui praebet aquam; post hunc quoque potus,
> condita cum verax aperit praecordia Liber:
> hic tibi comis et urbanus liberque videtur
> infesto nigris . . .
>   mentio siquae
> de Capitolini furtis iniecta Petilli
> te coram fuerit, defendas, ut tuus est mos:
> 'me Capitolinus convictore usus amicoque
> a puero est causaque mea permulta rogatus
> fecit et incolumis laetor quod vivit in urbe;
> sed tamen admiror, quo pacto iudicium illud
> fugerit'.

(The man who gnaws at his friend behind his back and fails
to defend him when blamed by another, who goes for men's
easy laughs and a reputation for wit, who can make up
what he has not seen and cannot keep quiet about what
has been entrusted to him: that man is black-hearted;
Roman, be on your guard against him. You may often see
twelve men dining, four to a couch, and one of them will
love to besprinkle everyone indiscriminately with his malice,
except for his host, though later he will attack him as well
when he is drunk and truthful Bacchus opens the recesses
of his heart. And to you, the enemy of the black-hearted,
he seems pleasant, witty and free-spoken. . . . If some

mention were made in your presence of Petillius Capitolinus
the embezzler, you would defend him in your usual way:
'I have been the comrade and friend of Capitolinus from
boyhood, and when I've asked him, he has done me many
a good turn, and I'm delighted that he's living safely in
Rome. At the same time I just wonder how his acquittal
was managed that time.')

It is against the background of this picture of Roman social
life that we should read the poet's reply to the proposal of his
persistent companion in 1.9 that he should help the poet displace
other members of Maecenas' circle of friends (48–52):

> 'non isto vivimus illic,
> quo tu rere, modo; domus hac nec purior ulla est
> nec magis his aliena malis; nil mi officit, inquam,
> ditior hic aut est quia doctior; est locus uni
> cuique suus.'

('We don't live there in the way that you think. There isn't
anywhere a more upright house or one more averse from
such behaviour. It doesn't hurt me if another among us is
richer or more learned than I. Each and every one has his
own place.')

This satire gives vivid expression to the contrast between the
private realm inhabited sometimes by himself alone and sometimes
as well by Maecenas and other friends and on the other hand
the mundane world of opportunism and competition in self-
advancement. Walking along the Sacred Way, the poet carries
about with him, as it were, his private domain, only to have it
invaded as his hand is seized (*arrepta manu*, 4); later (45–8) the
whole circle of Maecenas is under attack. It is perhaps permissible
to raise the question whether the final incident of the satire, the arrest
of the poet's companion, has a deeper significance than might at
first appear. The threat to the circle of Maecenas is removed through
the intervention of the law, which rescues the poet without even
his invoking its aid. Is the poet, unconsciously no doubt, pointing
to the power which lay behind the good taste and relaxed civility
of the circle? Does the arrest symbolize the confidence of an
establishment group that its position and interests will be maintained and defended from without?

In the countryside, however, the newly established master of the Sabine farm discovered, or rather perhaps re-discovered, another part of that private domain, one moreover which at the time seemed immune from undermining or attack. None of the brittleness which appears in the account of the visit of Maecenas and his friends to Nasidienus (II.8) can be detected in the picture of social life which emerges from II.2 and II.6. In II.2 the country-man Ofellus tells how if a friend who had not visited him for a long time arrived or if he was joined by a neighbour on a rainy day when work was impossible, he would serve his guest with a meal of chicken and kid, followed by raisins, nuts, figs and wine (118–25). The satire consists largely in an exposition of the homespun philosophy of Ofellus (*quae praecepit Ofellus/rusticus, abnormis sapiens crassaque Minerva*, 2–3), and it is tempting to suppose that Ofellus was accustomed at such meals to subject his guests to harangues rather like the satire itself. Certainly in the poet's account of the *cenae* which took place on his Sabine farm, philosophic discussion as well as improving fable have a place. These are open and tolerant occasions: his slaves as well as his friends partake of food, and no 'crazy rules' bind the drinkers as each takes wine at the strength which pleases him (II.6.65–70). Good sense is talked in this relaxed atmosphere (70–9):

> ergo
> sermo oritur, non de villis domibusve alienis,
> nec male necne Lepos saltet; sed, quod magis ad nos
> pertinet et nescire malum est, agitamus, utrumne
> divitiis homines an sint virtute beati,
> quidve ad amicitias, usus rectumne, trahat nos
> et quae sit natura boni summumque quid eius.
> Cervius haec inter vicinus garrit anilis
> ex re fabellas. siquis nam laudat Arelli
> sollicitas ignarus opes, sic incipit: 'olim . . .

(And so talk begins, not about other men's farms or
houses, nor whether Lepos is or is not a poor dancer.
We discuss matters of more relevance to us, about which it
would be wrong to be ignorant: whether it is riches or
virtue which makes men happy, whether it is utility or
goodness that draws us into friendship, what the nature of
the good is and what the supreme good. Between-whiles my

neighbour Cervius rattles on telling old wives' tales that
have a good deal of relevance. Thus if anyone extols the
wealth of Arellius without knowing about the worry that
goes with it, he begins like this: 'Once upon a time . . .')

Whether the friends (*mei*, 65) include sophisticates like the poet
himself or are all country folk like Cervius is not clear, but the
example of Ofellus should warn us against supposing that
ethical discussion, albeit *crassa Minerva*, was beyond the capacity
of a rustic gathering. In any case a firm line of demarcation is
drawn between Rome and the country, and only the poet is said
to cross it (16). Maecenas is firmly located in Rome. When the
poet is there, he still finds joy in being known as the great man's
friend, but it is a joy that is blended with much that is irritating
and tiresome (32–4). Later, in the *Odes*, he will write poems in
which his role will be to draw congenial companions from
✓ Rome in order to have them with him in the country, the girl
Tyndaris in 1.17 and Maecenas himself in III.29. And later still,
in the seventh epistle, that line of demarcation between town (and
Maecenas) and country (and Horace) becomes a fissure parting
the two as the poet assigns to himself and Maecenas the roles
respectively of ageing dependant and great friend in a discussion
of the ethical issues which arise when the dependant is drawn
away from the side of his friend in order to seek the peace of the
countryside. [3] Maecenas is there placed unambiguously outside the
poet's private realm, in which ethical principles have come to
play a dominant and demanding part.

Madness

Though this world of self and society is not unflawed, it is
nevertheless fundamentally sane. There have been satirists,
however, whose vision of society has been very different. For
Horace's contemporary Varro in his Menippean satire *Eumenides*,
for Juvenal in many of his satires and for Swift in the third book
of *Gulliver's Travels* the whole world is mad. [4] Probably every
satirist feels the attraction of some vision of madness enthroned,
but many have doubtless felt that it would represent too great a
distortion of reality to be made the basis of their work.

Horace was one of these. He entertained the idea, but never

really committed himself to it. Discontent and avarice are universal (I.I.I ff.; 108 ff.), and the majority of men are in various ways blameworthy (I.4.24 ff.), but nowhere in Book I is there an assertion that madness is universal. The poet seems rather in these early satires to have wished to show that one particular vice, sexual misconduct, bears the marks of madness. It alone among the vices mentioned in 1.4 is described as *insania* (27), and in 1.2 unbridled passion, whether for freedwomen or matrons, is equally insane (48–9). The craziness of adultery is suggested towards the end of the satire, where the poet's relaxed lovemaking is contrasted with the uncertainty, danger and indignity suffered by the adulterer (125 ff.).

In the second book Horace twice chose themes which lent themselves to the presentation of the world in terms of a single damning vision. Among the paradoxes in which the Stoics dealt were two which declared that all men with the exception of the sage are mad and enslaved. II.7 is largely devoted to the latter proposition, which forms the basis of a harangue directed at the poet by his slave Davus, who has picked up his knowledge of Stoicism from a slave employed as doorman by the philosopher Crispinus. Because of the personal relationship between Davus and his master, the satire hardly possesses the universal scope of the paradox upon which it is based. The kind of enslavement with which Davus is most concerned is sexual (46–71; 89–94). At one point he comes close to suggesting that we are all adulterers. Having reversed the position at the end of 1.2 – the poet no longer enjoys an 'easy and available love' (1.2.119), but now runs all the risks and discomfort of adultery – Davus finally acknowledges the poet's protests (II.7.72–4):

> 'non sum moechus' ais. neque ego hercule fur, ubi vasa
> praetereo sapiens argentea. tolle periclum:
> iam vaga prosiliet frenis natura remotis.

> (You say, 'I'm not an adulterer.' No, and I'm not a thief
> when I sensibly pass a silver vessel by. But remove the
> danger, and then, when the bridle is off, nature will leap
> forward ready to roam.)

Everyone then is actually or potentially a slave to adulterous passion. (Perhaps one should say that every man is since in

Horace the sexuality of women is a theme only of the *Epodes* and *Odes*.)

It was, however, in II.3 that Horace created on a scale to which he aspired in no other satire a true world of madness. The theme, that almost everyone is mad, is once again aggressively presented by a speaker possessing little intrinsic authority, a bankrupt converted to Stoicism who for the most part repeats the words spoken to him by the philosopher Stertinius which led to his conversion. The great length of this verbatim report of Stertinius' sermon (258 lines) goes far towards conveying an impression of the universality of madness, and the variety of forms which it can take is emphasized by the range of character and situation exhibited in the anecdotes and other illustrative material which form the most striking feature of the satire. The main part of Stertinius' discourse is arranged in sections, each devoted to a vice, indulgence in which is shown to be a mark of madness. They are avarice (82–157), pride (158–223), extravagance (224–46), love (247–80) and superstition (281–95). Many of the anecdotes seem to be located in Rome, but one is set in Canusium, a town not far from Horace's native Venusia in southern Italy, one is about a Greek philosopher in north Africa, and two tell of characters from Greek myth. There is besides a passage which is not so much an anecdote as an evocation of a scene from the timeless world of Roman comedy (259–71). Out of this varied material the poet has created a veritable world of madness.

It would be a mistake to expect a tone of unrelieved gloom. Here for example, in Professor Rudd's prose translation,[5] is the story of Opimius, poor Mr Richly (142–57):

> pauper Opimius argenti positi intus et auri,
> qui Veientanum festis potare diebus
> Campana solitus trulla vappamque profestis,
> quondam lethargo grandi est oppressus, ut heres
> iam circum loculos et clavis laetus ovansque
> curreret. hunc medicus multum celer atque fidelis
> excitat hoc pacto: mensam poni iubet atque
> effundi saccos nummorum, accedere pluris
> ad numerandum: hominem sic erigit; addit et illud:
> 'ni tua custodis, avidus iam haec auferet heres.'
> 'men vivo?' 'ut vivas igitur, vigila. hoc age.' 'quid vis?'

'deficient inopem venae te, ni cibus atque
ingens accedit stomacho fultura ruenti.
tu cessas? agedum sume hoc tisanarium oryzae.'
'quanti emptae?' 'parvo.' 'quanti ergo?' 'octussibus.' 'eheu,
quid refert, morbo an furtis pereamque rapinis?'

(Mr Richly, a poor man in spite of all the silver and gold
which he had stored away, used to drink cheap Veientine
wine from a cheap Campanian mug. That was on holidays;
on working days he drank fermented must. Once he was
sunk in so deep a coma that his heir was already running
round the chests and keys in triumphant joy. The doctor,
who was a loyal fellow with really quick reactions, roused
him by this method: he had a table brought; then he ordered
some bags of coins to be poured out and several people to
step forward and count them. After bringing the patient to
in this way he added 'If you don't watch your money, your
greedy heir will make off with it at any moment.' 'Over my
dead body!' 'All right then, wake up and stay alive. Here.'
'What's this?' 'Your pulse is dangerously low. Your system
is running down. It needs food and a really strong tonic.
What are you waiting for? Come on, take a sip of this rice
gruel.' 'How much was it?' 'Oh, not much.' 'Well *how*
much then?' 'A bob.' 'Ah dear me! What difference does
it make whether I die from illness or from theft and pillage?')

This story comes second in an almost unbroken sequence of
seven which runs from line 128 to 246 and places before the
reader a well-judged variety of character, place and time. Everywhere madness or the threat of it is present. The first draws a
grimly paradoxical contrast between the behaviour of the mad
matricide Orestes and supposedly sane Romans. After Opimius
comes a brilliant portrait of a sensible Italian bourgeois, aware of
the temptations which will face his sons. Next a contrast is drawn
between the harmless behaviour of the mad Ajax and the murder-
ousness of the supposedly sane Agamemnon. Lastly, three
anecdotes about luxury are drawn from *la dolce vita* of contemporary Rome.

After reading about Mr Richly, it seems appropriate to look at the other Italian story, equally lively though very differently organized (168–81):

> Servius Oppidius Canusi duo praedia, dives
> antiquo censu, gnatis divisse duobus
> fertur et hoc moriens pueris dixisse vocatis
> ad lectum: 'postquam te talos, Aule, nucesque
> ferre sinu laxo, donare et ludere vidi,
> te, Tiberi, numerare, cavis abscondere tristem,
> extimui, ne vos ageret vesania discors,
> tu Nomentanum, tu ne sequerere Cicutam.
> quare per divos oratus uterque Penatis
> tu cave ne minuas, tu ne maius facias id
> quod satis esse putat pater et natura coercet.
> praeterea ne vos titillet gloria, iure
> iurando obstringam ambo: uter aedilis fueritve
> vestrum praetor, is intestabilis et sacer esto.'

(It is said that Servius Oppidius, a man of ancient wealth, divided two estates at Canusium between his two sons and that calling them to his death-bed he spoke these words: 'I've noticed that you, Aulus, carry your dice and nuts about rather carelessly and that you give them away and gamble with them. And I've noticed you, Tiberius, glumly counting yours and hiding them in a hole. Now I've come to fear greatly that the two of you will be driven by opposite kinds of madness, with you, Aulus, imitating the spendthrift Nomentanus and you, Tiberius, Cicuta the money-lender. Accordingly I beseech you both by our household gods, you, Aulus, not to diminish and you, Tiberius, not to increase what your father thinks sufficient and what nature prescribes as a limit. Furthermore to prevent you thrilling to fame's caress, I shall bind you both by an oath: whichever of you shall be aedile or praetor shall be execrated and accursed.')

Arising from this mention of magistracies, there follows a vivid picture of a crazy politician trying to cut a *bella figura* before the people and losing his patrimony in the process (182–6):

'in cicere atque faba bona tu perdasque lupinis,
latus ut in circo spatiere et aeneus ut stes,
nudus agris, nudus nummis, insane, paternis;
scilicet ut plausus quos fert Agrippa feras tu,
astuta ingenuum volpes imitata leonem?'

('Are you to waste your substance buying peanuts for the
voters? Are you to be stripped of your father's fields and
coin, madman, so that you may stroll across the circus
grandly dressed and stand there too, cast in bronze, like a
sly fox playing the part of the noble lion in order (need I
say?) to win such applause as Agrippa enjoys?')

The mythological pieces both offer a novel view of a familiar
story. In the first, which belongs to the discussion of avarice, it is
pointed out that a man who pelted the populace or his own slaves
with stones would be regarded as insane. But is one who strangles
his wife or poisons his mother (the motive is doubtless profit from
a will) in his right mind? Mention of the killing of a mother
brings to mind the most notorious matricide, Orestes. The
Roman murderer would claim that he should not be regarded as a
second Orestes: after all that murder was committed with a sword,
and it happened at Argos. Tradition said that after the crime
Orestes became mad, but another view is possible (134–41):

an tu reris eum occisa insanisse parente
ac non ante malis dementem actum Furiis quam
in matris iugulo ferrum tepefecit acutum?
quin, ex quo est habitus male tutae mentis Orestes,
nil sane fecit quod tu reprehendere possis:
non Pyladen ferro violare aususve sororem
Electran, tantum maledicit utrique vocando
hanc Furiam, hunc aliud, iussit quod splendida bilis.

(Do you believe that he went mad after the killing of his
parent and that he had not been raving and driven by those
damnable Furies before he warmed his sword in his
mother's throat? Why, from the time he began to be
regarded as of unsound mind, Orestes did not do
anything at all you could find fault with. He did not dare
attack Pylades or his sister Electra with his sword, but

merely cursed each of them, calling her a Fury and him something else suggested by his blazing anger.)

The other mythological passage does not juxtapose past and present in this way, but contrasts instead two events connected with the Trojan War, the apparent madness of Ajax before Troy and the sacrifice by the apparently sane Agamemnon of his daughter Iphigeneia in order to still the contrary winds which were preventing the Greek fleet from sailing for Troy. The episode is presented dramatically with two speakers, Agamemnon and a *plebeius*, a common soldier in the Greek army, we may suppose, who, however, displays some of the features of those Stoic or Cynic sages who in literature and in fact confronted kings and tyrants (187–207)

> nequis humasse velit Aiacem, Atrida, vetas cur?
> 'rex sum – ' nil ultra quaero plebeius. ' – et aequam
> rem imperito, ac sicui videor non iustus, inulto
> dicere quod sentit permitto.' maxime regum,
> di tibi dent capta classem reducere Troia.
> ergo consulere et mox respondere licebit?
> 'consule.' cur Aiax, heros ab Achille secundus,
> putescit, totiens servatis clarus Achivis,
> gaudeat ut populus Priami Priamusque inhumato,
> per quem tot iuvenes patrio caruere sepulcro?
> 'mille ovium insanus morti dedit, inclitum Ulixen
> et Menelaum una mecum se occidere clamans.'
> tu cum pro vitula statuis dulcem Aulide natam
> ante aras spargisque mola caput, inprobe, salsa,
> rectum animi servas? 'quorsum?' insanus quid enim Aiax
> fecit? cum stravit ferro pecus, abstinuit vim
> uxore et gnato; mala multa precatus Atridis
> non ille aut Teucrum aut ipsum violavit Ulixen.
> 'verum ego, ut haerentis adverso litore navis
> eriperem, prudens placavi sanguine divos.'
> nempe tuo, furiose. 'meo, sed non furiosus.'

('Why, son of Atreus, do you forbid the burial of Ajax?'
'I am king . . .'
'As a man of the people I ask no further.'
'. . . and my commands are just. If I appear to anyone to be unjust, I allow him to speak his mind with impunity.'

'Greatest of kings, may the gods grant you to take Troy and lead back your fleet. So question and answer will be allowed?'

'Put your question.'

'Why does Ajax, who was second to Achilles among the heroes and who won fame for saving the Achaeans so many times, why does he lie rotting so that Priam and Priam's people rejoice that he is unburied who deprived so many of their warriors of burial in the tombs of their ancestors?'

'In his madness he put one thousand sheep to death, crying out that he was killing Ulysses, Menelaus and me.'

'Were *you* in your right mind when at Aulis you placed your sweet daughter instead of a calf before the altar and shamelessly sprinkled her head with sacrificial meal?'

'What do you mean?'

'What after all did Ajax do in his madness? When he laid the sheep low with his sword, he abstained from violence against his wife and son. He uttered many a curse against the sons of Atreus, but he did not harm Teucer or even Ulysses.'

'But it was in order to drag my ships away as they clung to the unfriendly shore that I deliberately appeased the gods with blood'.

'That blood of course was your own, madman.'

'It was, but I was not mad.')

Agamemnon's denial is now refuted: anyone whose mental images are contrary to reality is regarded as mad; thus Ajax showed that he was mad when he mistook the innocent sheep for his enemies, but did not Agamemnon exhibit a similar confusion? A fantastic analogy drawn from Roman society makes this clear (214–20):

> siquis lectica nitidam gestare amet agnam,
> huic vestem ut gnatae, paret ancillas, paret aurum,
> Rufam aut Pusillam appellet fortique marito
> destinet uxorem: interdicto huic omne adimat ius
> praetor et ad sanos abeat tutela propinquos.
> quid, siquis gnatam pro muta devovet agna,
> integer est animi?

(If a man were in the habit of having a sleek ewe-lamb
carried about in a sedan-chair, if he provided her, just like a
daughter, with clothes, maids and gold, called her Rufa or
Pusilla and betrothed her to a brave husband, he would be
made subject to an order from the praetor depriving him of
all his legal rights, and he would become a ward in the care
of his sane kinsfolk. Now if another man in place of a
dumb lamb consecrates his daughter for sacrifice, is he of
sound mind?)

Of the three anecdotes which follow and make up the section
on the subject of luxury, the first and longest offers a brilliant
account of an aspect of Rome which the passages about the city
considered earlier scarcely acknowledged. Nomentanus has
just inherited a fortune, and the purveyors of luxury and vice
come crowding to his door (224–38):

> nunc age luxuriam et Nomentanum arripe mecum.
> vincet enim stultos ratio insanire nepotes.
> hic simul accepit patrimoni mille talenta,
> edicit, piscator uti, pomarius, auceps,
> unguentarius ac Tusci turba inpia vici,
> cum scurris fartor, cum Velabro omne macellum
> mane domum veniant. quid tum? venere frequentes,
> verba facit leno: 'quidquid mihi, quidquid et horum
> cuique domi est, id crede tuum et vel nunc pete vel cras.'
> accipe quid contra haec iuvenis responderit aequus.
> 'in nive Lucana dormis ocreatus, ut aprum
> cenem ego; tu piscis hiberno ex aequore verris.
> segnis ego, indignus qui tantum possideam; aufer,
> sume tibi decies; tibi tantundem; tibi triplex,
> unde uxor media currit de nocte vocata.'

(Come now and join me in assailing luxury and
Nomentanus, for reason will prove that spendthrifts are
crazy fools. As soon as Nomentanus had inherited one
thousand talents, he issued instructions that fisherman,
fruiterer, bird-catcher and perfumer, the whole ungodly
mob from Etruscan Street, the poultry-fattener and hangers-
on, the whole meat-market and the population of the
Velabrum should all come to his house early in the morning.

And then? They came in droves with the pander as
spokesman: 'Be assured', said he, 'that anything I or any of
us has at home is yours. Ask for it now or tomorrow.' Here
is the reply of that fair-minded young man: 'You sleep in
your huntsman's leggings amid the snows of Lucania so
that I may have boar for dinner. And *you* sweep fish from
the stormy sea. But I am so lazy I don't deserve my wealth.
Take it away. Here's a million sesterces for you; and the
same for you; and for you, whose wife comes running
from your side when she gets that midnight call, three
million.')

This passage, which apart from the reference to the *unguentarius*
(228) does not look beyond the resources of Italy, is worth
comparing with one written a century or so later, where a man
of cosmic vision sees Rome as the abode of luxury served by the
seafaring men and traders of the world (Revelation, 18:11–17):[6]

The merchants of the earth also will weep and mourn for
her, because no one any longer buys their cargoes, cargoes
of gold and silver, jewels and pearls, cloths of purple and
scarlet, silks and fine linens; all kinds of scented woods,
ivories, and every sort of thing made of costly woods,
bronze, iron, or marble; cinnamon and spice, incense,
perfumes and frankincense; wine, oil, flour and wheat,
sheep and cattle, horses, chariots, slaves, and the lives
of men. 'The fruit you longed for', they will say, 'is gone
from you; all the glitter and the glamour are lost, never to be
yours again!' The traders in all these wares, who gained their
wealth from her, will stand at a distance for horror at her
torment, weeping and mourning and saying, 'Alas, alas for
the great city, that was clothed in fine linen and purple and
scarlet, bedizened with gold and jewels and pearls! Alas
that in one hour so much wealth should be laid waste!'

While the sermon in II.3 expresses by virtue of its length
and variety the universality of madness, it is possible to suggest
also its crazy intensity by describing in detail the career of one
who devotes himself unsparingly to the practice of a single vice.
Horace does this in II.5, where he deals fancifully with a very
contemporary theme, legacy-hunting, discussing it in a setting

which could scarcely be more remote, the visit of Ulysses to the underworld and his meeting there with the seer Teiresias. Learning that he is fated to return destitute to Ithaca, Ulysses asks how he is to restore his fortune. Teiresias does not provide a general answer, but plunges into detail. Any delicacies that come to hand, a thrush for example, are to 'wing their way' to a wealthy old man. Walking with him, Ulysses must respectfully take the outside of the pavement even if his companion is a perjurer, of low birth, a fratricide or a runaway slave. At first the hero recoils from the suggestion, but then swallows his pride and asks for more instruction. Only now does Teiresias become explicit: Ulysses must fish everywhere for the wills of old men and not give up hope if one or two crafty ones take the bait, but not the hook. It is a life of ingratiation, and one approach is to make use of the law-courts (27–39; 42–4):

> magna minorve foro si res certabitur olim,
> vivet uter locuples sine gnatis, inprobus, ultro
> qui meliorem audax vocet in ius, illius esto
> defensor; fama civem causaque priorem
> sperne, domi si gnatus erit fecundave coniunx.
> 'Quinte' puta aut 'Publi' – gaudent praenomine molles
> auriculae – 'tibi me virtus tua fecit amicum.
> ius anceps novi, causas defendere possum;
> eripiet quivis oculos citius mihi quam te
> contemptum cassa nuce pauperet; haec mea cura est,
> nequid tu perdas neu sis iocus.' ire domum atque
> pelliculam curare iube; fi cognitor ipse,
> persta atque obdura . . .
> 'nonne vides' aliquis cubito stantem prope tangens
> inquiet, 'ut patiens, ut amicis aptus, ut acer?'
> plures adnabunt thynni et cetaria crescent.

(If there is a case, great or small, being tried in the courts some time and if one of the parties is a childless rich man, a villain who has the nerve without provocation to drag a better man into court, you must become the rich man's supporter. If the other has a son or fruitful wife at home, have no thought for him even though his reputation and his case are better. 'Quintus' for example, you will say, or 'Publius', (his susceptible ears are delighted to hear the

first name) 'your merits have made me your friend. I know
the ambiguities of the law, and I can defend a case. I'd sooner
have anyone tear my eyes out than that he should despise
you and rob you of a nutshell. It is my concern that you
should suffer no loss nor become a laughing-stock.' Tell
him to go home and look after his precious self. Become
his representative yourself, stand firm and endure. . . . And
someone will nudge his neighbour and say, 'Don't you see
how painstaking he is, how he conforms to the needs of his
friends, how keen he is?' More tunnies will come swimming
in, and your fishponds will grow more crowded.)

There is no need to confine oneself to pursuing the childless.
A rich man with a delicate son is a suitable quarry. If Ulysses
succeeds in being made 'second heir' and 'if some chance carries
the boy off to Hades' (an ironical supposition – Ulysses will
doubtless help him on his way there), then he will occupy the
vacant place. Later on he is told how to vary his approach according to the temperament of his victim (90–7):

> difficilem et morosum offendet garrulus: ultra
> 'non' 'etiam' sileas; Davus sis comicus atque
> stes capite obstipo, multum similis metuenti.
> obsequio grassare; mone, si increbruit aura,
> cautus uti velet carum caput; extrahe turba
> oppositis umeris; aurem substringe loquaci.
> inportunus amat laudari: donec 'ohe iam'
> ad caelum manibus sublatis dixerit, urge.

(A chatterbox will give offence to one who is surly and
morose; say nothing to him except 'Yes' and 'No', and be
like Davus in the play, looking apprehensive and keeping
your head bent. Show respect and concern as you make
your approach: if the breeze freshens, tell him to take care
and cover his precious head; get him out of a press of
people by using your shoulders; if he talks a lot, listen
with your hand to your ear. If he is a demanding type who
loves to be praised, ply him with praise until he raises his
hands to heaven and says 'Steady on'.)

Even after the victim's death pretence must continue. Ulysses
must hide his delight when the will is read, must express his

regret at the death of his friend and weep a tear if possible – and not forget to assess the possibilities of finding another quarry among his coheirs (106–9):

> siquis
> forte coheredum senior male tussiet, huic tu
> dic, ex parte tua seu fundi sive domus sit
> emptor, gaudentem nummo te addicere.

(If one of them should chance to be rather old and with a bad cough, and if he would like to buy a farm or house forming part of your legacy, tell him you would be glad to make it over to him for a nominal amount.)

So this madness is a *perpetuum mobile* as the death of one quarry leads to the pursuit of another, and Teiresias can bring his address to an end only by breaking off abruptly (109–10):

> sed me
> imperiosa trahit Proserpina: vive valeque.

(But stern Proserpine drags me away. Live and fare well.)

Art

In certain parts of Book 1 the act of writing poetry seems to fill a very marginal place in the poet's disposal of his time. It receives the merest mention in the description in 1.6 of his contented life at Rome (122–3):

> ad quartam iaceo; post hanc vagor aut ego lecto
> aut scripto quod me tacitum iuvet unguor olivo.

(I lie in bed until 10 o'clock. Then either I take an aimless stroll or after reading or writing something to please my silent hours I rub myself with olive oil.)

His saying so little here about his own poetry is probably not unconnected with the fact that the criticisms of himself which he discusses in the satire bear upon the social success which he, a freedman's son, has enjoyed in being given a high military command during the Civil Wars and later in becoming an intimate friend of Maecenas. He says nothing of criticism directed against him as an upstart who presumed to write satire. Yet he may very

well have been attacked on this score, for although the history of
Latin poetry in the Republican and Augustan periods shows it
to have been in general a *carrière ouverte aux talents*, it must have
seemed to many that 'rubbing down the city with salt' (1.10.4)
was an activity to which only the well-born like Lucilius or Varro
had a right to aspire.[7]

While 1.6 is thus primarily concerned with the poet's social
position, 1.4 deals with criticism of his poetry. Yet even here,
when he comes to speak of his way of life, the actual composition
of his poems seems to be of minor importance. Answering the
charge that he is too outspoken, the poet declares that the
freedom of his comment derives from his father, who taught
moral lessons by pointing to examples in society. As a result of
this training his own vices are modest ones, and even these have
perhaps been cut back by time, outspoken friends and his own
moral pondering. He continues (133–42):

> neque enim, cum lectulus aut me
> porticus excepit, desum mihi. 'rectius hoc est;
> hoc faciens vivam melius; sic dulcis amicis
> occurram; hoc quidam non belle: numquid ego illi
> inprudens olim faciam simile?' haec ego mecum
> conpressis agito labris; ubi quid datur oti,
> inludo chartis. hoc est mediocribus illis
> ex vitiis unum; cui si concedere nolis,
> multa poetarum veniat manus, auxilio quae
> sit mihi.

(When I find myself on my couch or walking in a colonnade,
I do not neglect my well-being. With my lips closed I turn
these thoughts over in my mind: 'This is the more correct
course. If I do that, my life will be better. In this way I
shall be regarded with affection by my friends. It wasn't
pretty when X acted in that way; would I ever be so
foolish as to act similarly?' When I'm given some leisure
(*quid oti*), I amuse myself with my writing (*inludo chartis*).
That is one of those modest vices, and if you won't forgive
me for it, a great band of poets will come to help me.

Taking second place to the weighing of alternative ways of
behaviour, writing belongs to the sphere of leisure (*otium*), which

means that it is in no sense a serious or demanding business (*negotium*). His refusal earlier (39–62) to claim for his satires the name of poetry or for himself the name of poet is in harmony with this rather dismissive attitude to the activity of writing.

But the poet is an ironist, and in making statements about matters that mean a great deal to him he is apt to say much less than he means. That he regarded the writing of satire as a demanding art becomes clear in the latest of the satires of Book I, the tenth. He recalls that in 1.4 he had praised his great predecessor Lucilius for his aggressive manner, but he now asserts that the genre is governed by canons which Lucilius failed to observe (5–17):

> nec tamen hoc tribuens dederim quoque cetera; nam sic
> et Laberi mimos ut pulchra poemata mirer.
> ergo non satis est risu diducere rictum
> auditoris; et est quaedam tamen hic quoque virtus.
> est brevitate opus, ut currat sententia neu se
> inpediat verbis lassas onerantibus auris,
> et sermone opus est modo tristi, saepe iocoso,
> defendente vicem modo rhetoris atque poetae,
> interdum urbani, parcentis viribus atque
> extenuantis eas consulto. ridiculum acri
> fortius et melius magnas plerumque secat res.
> illi, scripta quibus comoedia prisca viris est,
> hoc stabant, hoc sunt imitandi.

(But while granting him this, I would not at the same time allow him all the other qualities, for if I did that, I should have to admire the mimes of Laberius also as beautiful poems. So it is not enough to make your listener laugh and bare his teeth like an animal – though there is a certain merit in that too. There is need for brevity so that the thought may run along and not get entangled with words that weigh down and weary the ear. There is need for language that is at one time severe, often light-hearted, taking at one time the part of orator and poet, at other times that of the man of wit who husbands his strength and deliberately refrains from using it to the full. Quite often great issues are settled better and more forcefully by an appeal to laughter than by severity. The great men who

wrote Old Comedy based themselves on that, and in that
they are to be imitated.)

This must be regarded as an implicit statement of the artistic
principles according to which Horace writes satire. Professor
Rudd has shown how Lucilius failed to meet these require-
ments, but it is perhaps also worth while looking at Horace's
work in the light of this statement.[8]

(1) *So it is not enough to make your listener laugh and bare his teeth
like an animal – though there is a certain merit in that too.* Coarse and
vulgar humour is to have a place, but a relatively minor one.
The main sources of this kind of humour have in many societies
been man's sexual and excretory functions. The latter are referred
to in isolation only at 1.8.38 and 46–7, where the speaker is the
shameless god Priapus. Elsewhere, at II.7.52 and 1.2.44, verbs
having excretory senses are used with sexual connotations. 1.2
and II.7 are in fact the only satires which make use of the humorous
potentialities of sex. The language is often coarse (*permolere,
testis caudamque salacem, muttonis, tument inguina, futuo*), sometimes
rather elegant and free from this kind of vocabulary (*mea cum
conferbuit ira, simul ac venas inflavit taetra libido*), or an expression
may blend coarseness with wit or elegance as in *cunni albi* or
(II.7.47–50):

> sub clara nuda lucerna
> quaecumque excepit turgentis verbera caudae
> clunibus aut agitavit equum lasciva supinum.

(2) *There is need for brevity so that the thought may run along and not
get entangled with words that weigh down and weary the ear.* The end
of the poet's account of his first meeting with Maecenas illustrates this quality well (1.6.60–2):

> respondes, ut tuus est mos,
> pauca; abeo, et revocas nono post mense iubesque
> esse in amicorum numero.

(Your answer was brief, as usual. I went away and after
nine months you called me back and bade me be one of
your friends.)

Such simple brevity could not, however, hold the reader's interest
for long, and the greater elaboration of the lines which precede

is more typical of the poet's straightforward and still basically simple and brief manner (1.6.54–60):

> nulla etenim mihi te fors obtulit: optimus olim
> Vergilius, post hunc Varius dixere, quid essem.
> ut veni coram, singultim pauca locutus –
> infans namque pudor prohibebat plura profari –
> non ego me claro natum patre, non ego circum
> me Satureiano vectari rura caballo,
> sed quod eram narro.

(It was no chance which brought you to me: one time
good Virgil and after him Varius told you what I was.
When I came before you, I gulped and said little –
speechless embarrassment stopped me saying more. I didn't
tell you I was the son of a distinguished father or that
I rode round my estate on a Satureian cob – no, I told you
what I was.)

There are occasions of course when the poet is deliberately long-winded. In telling the rather jejune story of Persius and Rupilius Rex, for example, he allows for comic effect a digression eight lines long and written in an elaborate epic style to delay the beginning of the narrative (1.7.10–18).

(3) *There is need for language that is at one time severe, often light-hearted, taking at one time the part of orator and poet, at other times that of the man of wit who husbands his strength and deliberately refrains from using it to the full.*

(a) *Severity of language.* This refers to the element of invective. It covers condemnatory words like *moechus* and *nebulo*, but also more poetic effects such as the scornful alliteration and assonance of (II.3.243–5):

> Quinti progenies Arri, par nobile fratrum
> nequitia et nugis pravorum et amore gemellum
> luscinias soliti inpenso prandere coemptas.

(The progeny of Quintus Arrius, that notorious pair of
playboy twins, passionately devoted to what's bad, who go
in for lunching on nightingales purchased at a prodigious
price.)

88

(b) *Light-hearted language.* This is well exemplified in 1.9 with its urbane self-mockery. In the following passage the poet hopes that his friend Aristius Fuscus will rescue him from his persistent companion, but Fuscus, a poker-faced schoolmaster, disappoints him, maliciously offering only a piece of pseudo-erudition as justification for his refusal to help (60–74):

> haec dum agit, ecce
> Fuscus Aristius occurrit, mihi carus et illum
> qui pulchre nosset. consistimus. 'unde venis' et
> 'quo tendis?' rogat et respondet. vellere coepi
> et pressare manu lentissima bracchia, nutans,
> distorquens oculos, ut me eriperet. male salsus
> ridens dissimulare; meum iecur urere bilis.
> 'certe nescio quid secreto velle loqui te
> aiebas mecum.' 'memini bene, sed meliore
> tempore dicam; hodie tricensima sabbata: vin tu
> curtis Iudaeis oppedere?' 'nulla mihi' inquam
> 'religio est.' 'at mi: sum paulo infirmior, unus
> multorum. ignosces; alias loquar.' huncine solem
> tam nigrum surrexe mihi! fugit inprobus ac me
> sub cultro linquit.

(While he's saying this, lo and behold, up comes Aristius Fuscus, a dear friend who knew my companion well. We stop. 'Where are you coming from and where are you off to?' he asks, and then he answers the same questions. I begin to pull and pinch his unfeeling arms, nodding and winking at him to rescue me. He laughed and with his misplaced sense of humour pretended not to understand. I boiled with anger. 'Surely', said I, 'there was something you said you wanted to discuss with me in private.' 'I haven't forgotten, but I'll mention it at a more suitable time. Today's the thirtieth Sabbath – do you want me to give offence to the circumcized Jews?' 'I've no scruples', I replied. 'But I have', said he. 'I'm rather less strong-minded, like many another. Please forgive me; another time.' To think that this day's dawn was so disastrous! Off with him, the unfeeling wretch, leaving me beneath the axe.)

(c) *Rhetorical and poetic language*. In the *Satires* high-flown language tends to be mock-solemn. An earlier passage in the same satire illustrates this (29–34):[9]

> confice; namque instat fatum mihi triste, Sabella
> quod puero cecinit divina mota anus urna:
> 'hunc neque dira venena nec hosticus auferet ensis
> nec laterum dolor aut tussis nec tarda podagra:
> garrulus hunc quando consumet cumque: loquaces,
> si sapiat, vitet, simul atque adoleverit aetas.'

(Finish me off. In truth there hangs over me that grim fate which a Samnite fortune-teller, shaking her urn, uttered to me when a boy: 'Neither deadly poison nor foeman's sword nor a pain in the side or a cough nor halting gout will carry off this boy. But there shall come a day when a chatterbox will destroy him. Once his years have reached maturity, let him, if he is wise, avoid the talkative.')

(d) *Urbane restraint*. Sometimes the poet refrains from impassioned denunciation and delivers instead a quick, deadly thrust.[10] A certain adulterer, he recalls in 1.2, was castrated (46):[11]

> 'iure' omnes; Galba negabat.
> ('Quite right too', everyone said – Galba disagreed.)

And in 1.4, in the course of an argument about the language of comedy and of real life, he deals a shrewd blow at a certain Pomponius. An imaginary interlocutor, objecting to the view that the speech of comedy differs from that of everyday life only in being metrical, refers to an episode where a comic character uses elevated language (48–52):

> 'at pater ardens
> saevit, quod meretrice nepos insanus amica
> filius uxorem grandi cum dote recuset,
> ebrius et, magnum quod dedecus, ambulet ante
> noctem cum facibus.'

('But you have the situation where a father is ablaze with rage because his spendthrift son, madly in love with a prostitute, refuses a wife with a rich dowry and disgraces himself utterly by going around drunk before nightfall and carrying a torch.')

The poet simultaneously answers the argument and discharges his shaft at Pomponius. It seems all the more cruel because Pomponius is not in exactly the same position as the young man in the play (52-3):

> numquid Pomponius istis
> audiret leviora, pater si viveret?

(Would Pomponius hear gentler words from *his* father if he were alive?)

Horace's setting up of these canons and his attempt to compose in accordance with them is evidence for a fundamentally serious and committed approach to the writing of satire. An expression like *ubi quid datur oti* belongs rather to the relaxed approach of a member of high society such as Lucilius than to a professional poet. Used by Horace, it must be regarded as ironical.

In II.I, where for the last time Horace discusses his writing of satire, the leisurely approach is nowhere to be found. Trebatius, the lawyer whom he consults about his poetic career, senses that he is possessed by a passion to write (*tantus amor scribendi*, 10). This, the poet later explains, is something personal to him; other men have other pursuits (24-9):

> quid faciam? saltat Milonius, ut semel icto
> accessit fervor capiti numerusque lucernis;
> Castor gaudet equis, ovo prognatus eodem
> pugnis; quot capitum vivunt, totidem studiorum
> milia: me pedibus delectat claudere verba
> Lucili ritu, nostrum melioris utroque.

(What am I to do? As soon as the wine's heat hits his head and he sees more lights than are there, Milonius must dance. Castor loves horses while his twin, born from the same egg, enjoys boxing. There are as many thousand pursuits as there are individuals. As for me, it's my delight to put words together in feet in the manner of Lucilius, a better man than either of us.)

Although he continues by singling out the self-revelation of Lucilius, the words *me . . . delectat* can be taken to apply in general to his own writing of satire. They offer the most satisfactory account of the basic impulse which led him to write. He is a satirist not because he wishes to reform society or to defend himself against his enemies, but because he enjoys making poetry with a peculiarly personal and intermittently aggressive tone. The satirist, it has been said, 'is stimulated by the incongruities of societies, he is infuriated or amused by them, and he ridicules them. Later, because men are expected to justify their actions, he rationalizes that his purpose was noble and virtuous.'[12] In 1.10 Horace had made the point that the genres of comedy, tragedy, epic and pastoral were already in the hands of gifted poets, and that this left him with satire, a kind of poetry which had not been composed with success since the days of Lucilius (40-8). This should not be dismissed as merely a piece of misleading irony or a compliment to four of his contemporaries. Genres were important in the ancient world, and a young poet with the itch to write might very well have been struck by the coincidence between the absence from contemporary literature of a successful writer of Lucilian satire and a tendency in himself to view the world with a critical eye. Horace's simultaneous commitment to the two aggressive genres of Archilochean iambus and Lucilian satire must surely, even when allowance has been made for the role of convention in the attitudes struck by satirist or iambographer, be indicative of a close affinity between himself and their combative spirit.

Notes

1 E. Doblhofer, *Die Augustuspanegyrik des Horaz in formalhistorischer Sicht*, Heidelberg, 1966, 17 ff.
2 S. Treggiari, *Roman Freedmen during the late Republic*, Oxford, 1969, 271-2.
3 M. J. McGann, *Studies in Horace's First Book of Epistles*, Brussels, 1969, 95-6; G. Williams, *Tradition and Originality in Roman Poetry*, Oxford, 1968, 19 ff., 566 ff.
4 L. Feinberg, *Introduction to Satire*, Ames, Iowa, 1967, 44 ff.
5 N. Rudd, *The Satires of Horace*, Cambridge, 1966, 188. Thanks are due to the translator and the publisher for permission to quote.
6 Revelation 18:11-17 is from the *New English Bible*, second edition © 1970 by permission of Oxford and Cambridge University Presses.
7 For two satirists who were freedmen see Suet. *Gramm.* 5 and 15 with Treggiari's discussion, op. cit., 114 and 119. While Pompeius Lenaeus defended his former master by attacking Sallust, who had criticized him, there is nothing to indicate that either freedman engaged in general

criticism of *mores* or political behaviour. It must, however, be emphasized that little is known about the writing of satire between Lucilius and Horace.

8 Rudd, op. cit., 97 ff. For some examples of Horace's putting principle into practice see also E. Fraenkel, *Horace*, Oxford, 1957, 81–2 and 108–9.

9 The passage has been discussed by Fraenkel, op. cit., 117–18. For a flash of high-flown panegyric set in an ironic context see II.2.13–15.

10 Cf. Fraenkel, op. cit., 85–6.

11 Galba was certainly an adulterer and very possible the *quidam* who had been castrated. It is doubtful whether Lejay was right in following the ancient commentators, who probably on the basis of *iure* alone held that Galba was a lawyer who allowed his private inclinations to affect his professional opinion.

12 Feinberg, op. cit., 12.

IV

Horace and the Verse Letter

O. A. W. Dilke

The verse letter as a literary form

Little attention has been paid to the form which Horace adopted when in 23 B.C. he laid down his 'Roman lyre'[1] and resumed the writing of hexameter poetry. *Sermones*, 'talks', is the word under which he seems to bracket his satires and epistles. Commentators, perhaps because of this bracketing, have been too inclined to ignore the epistolary background and tradition.[2]

The literary epistle, in its early prose form, was particularly associated with philosophy, to which Horace claimed now to be dedicating himself. Plato's letters[3] were chiefly linked with his desire to equate the philosopher with the king in the western Greek world. Since none of the prominent cities on the Greek mainland looked like welcoming a guiding hand from a philosopher, he tried casting his net wider, to the new world of Greater Greece. We do not possess the letters of Aristotle, of which Demetrius writes:[4] 'We shall now deal with the style of letter-writing, as this too requires the simple manner. Artemon, who edited the letters of Aristotle, says that letters and dialogues should be written in the same way, for a letter is like one side of a dialogue.' Demetrius himself thinks that, while this is largely true, a letter should be written more carefully than a dialogue. The editor of the collection, perhaps to be identified with Artemon of Cassandrea, added a commentary on the art of letter-writing.

Epicurus' letter to Menoeceus expounds his moral philosophy; it seems unlikely that Horace, despite his inclinations, was indebted to it. We hear also of collections of letters by Theophrastus, Arcesilaus and Carneades. There were even forgeries

of philosophical letters, such as those purporting to be by the
Cynic Diogenes. Physics, mathematics, and at a later date literary
criticism too contributed to this genre. We can imagine that an
offshoot of the philosophical epistle, the 'ingenious letters' of
Menippus of Gadara, noted for his serio-comic style (σπουδαιο-
γέλοιον),[5] may well have contributed to the development of
Horace's work. Cicero writes to Curio[6] that one of the types of
letter that he likes is the friendly, jocular type (*familiare et iocosum*).
This same jocular aspect occurred among other topics in the lost
correspondence of Augustus to Atticus.[7] We can sample some of
the humour from a letter of Augustus to Horace, containing the
sentence: 'You can write on a pint pot, so that the circumference
of your volume will be more elephantine, like your corporation.'[8]

Horace was not the first to write verse letters: he had at least
two predecessors in Latin literature. In 146 B.C. Sp. Mummius
wrote from Corinth, which his brother L. Mummius had just
conquered, *epistulas versiculis facetis ad familiares missas*, 'humorous
verse letters to his friends'.[9] This is a certain example by a
member of the Scipionic circle and a Stoic, but one which has
not survived at all, whereas the other is less certain. Lucilius,
whom Horace acknowledged as his master in satire, composed
the fifth book of his *Satires* about 117–16 B.C. In one poem of this
book[10] he complained to a friend that he was not visited by him
when he was ill, and continued:

> quo me habeam pacto, tam etsi non quaeris, docebo,
> quando in eo numero mansi quo in maxima non est
> pars hominum.

> (My state of health, although you do not ask,
> You shall be told, seeing that I have stayed
> In the minority of all mankind.)

If Lucilius had confined himself to his state of health, there would
be little likely similarity with Horace. But he proceeds to use the
verbs *nolueris* and *debueris* in close proximity (we can easily reproduce this play with 'wouldn't', and the opposite of *debueris*,
'shouldn't') and later has two more similar endings, *lerodes* and
meiraciodes (we could perhaps try at the effect with 'burlesque' and
'studentesque'). Lucilius professes impatience with his friend if
the latter criticizes this type of wording as artless and Isocratean.
Clearly the sense is not that Isocrates wrote letters like speeches,

but that he loved similar endings of this sort. The two Greek adjectives quoted above are no doubt intended to recall student humour of the writer's youth from Athens or Rhodes. This fragment shows that the poem, like others of Lucilius, digressed far beyond the point at issue.

Undoubtedly Lucilius' poem has influenced Horace, but Horace has been careful to avoid the mistake just mentioned. In the first four lines of *Epist.*, 1.16 he anticipates enquiry with the opening phrase:

> ne perconteris, fundus meus, optime Quincti,
> arvo pascat erum an bacis opulentet olivae,
> pomisne an pratis an amicta vitibus ulmo,
> scribetur tibi forma loquaciter et situs agri.

> (In case, my good friend Quinctius, you should ask
> Whether my farm is arable or makes
> Its master rich with olives or with apples,
> With pastures or with elm-trees clad in vines,
> I will describe for you loquaciously
> The site and the appearance of my farm.)

Horace, however, does not digress widely from his theme in order to return to it. His technique is to devote the following twelve lines to this geographical aspect,[11] which he then, however, leaves permanently in order to enter on his philosophical theme: is Quinctius really as happy as all Rome says he is?

Romans of the generation before Horace were great letter-writers, and the influence of some of the letters in Cicero's collection on Horace's verse letters can surely be discerned. A typical example of the business letter was one introducing a young man to a senior friend. This gives rise both to the elegant *Epist.*, 1.9, addressed to Tiberius, and to *Epist.*, 1.12.22–4, addressed to Agrippa's Sicilian manager, Iccius. Horace does not content himself with bald introductions. In the first of these two he makes an ethical point: where there is a conflict of duties, one must weigh them up and avoid the action which bears the greater blame. The second also achieves some elegance, by a metaphor suitable to a man who ran vast estates:

> vilis amicorum est annona, bonis ubi quid deest.

> (Friends turn out cheap when good men are in need.)

It must, nevertheless, be admitted that Horace did not attain the level of literary height that he might have if instead of concentrating on popular ethics, commenting on contemporary writers, and such themes he had aspired to the nobler thoughts of a prose writer of the calibre of Servius Sulpicius Rufus. In the most famous letter of this elevated type Sulpicius consoles Cicero for the loss of his daughter, Tullia. As he sailed past places like Megara, already a shadow of its former self (it still is today), he reflected on the downfall of great cities and the comparative insignificance of human tragedies. There is nothing like this in Horace's letters: it is perhaps instructive to see the quite different angles he has on Greek cities. *Epist.*, 1.11, addressed to Bullatius, reminisces on places in Asia Minor and adjacent islands which the poet had known while he was serving under Brutus, and argues against what sounds like a friend's genuine but 'castle in the air' plan to settle at Lebedos, a very small seaside place in Asia Minor.[12] *Epist.*, 1.2 recommends Homer as the ideal guide to human conduct. There are echoes of these topographical and literary reminiscences elsewhere, such as the queries on Julius Florus' journey past the Hellespont in *Epist.*, 1.3 and the reference to Telemachus' refusal of a present of horses in *Epist.*, 1.7. None of these allusions to Greece and to Greek literature is on anything like the same level as that of Sulpicius Rufus. Yet they do form part of the same literary tradition, represented both in its prose and verse forms.

The tradition is carried on by Ovid, who in his *Heroides*[13] embroidered on the literary framework of letter-writing to make his mythological heroes and heroines write to each other, and whose *Letters from the Black Sea* also preserve the elegiac form; by Seneca, who in each of his prose *Letters to Lucilius* briefly mentioned an incident or circumstance in order to build Stoic philosophy round it, often, like Horace, pouring scorn on current fashions; by Statius, who, among other *Silvae*,[14] wrote to his wife (*Silv.*, III.5) trying to persuade her to leave Rome and join him in Naples;[15] and by the younger Pliny, who polished his letters up carefully before publication, and liked including verse extracts in them.[16]

In the post-classical period the main exponents of the verse letter are Ausonius and Sidonius. Twenty-five of Ausonius' letters are preserved, some of them showing prose and verse,

Greek and Latin interspersed in the poet's learned manner. The macaronic had been used by Lucilius, but was carefully avoided by Horace and is not found in extant Golden Age poetry. Sidonius wrote a large number of prose letters, well polished up for publication in Plinian style and each confined to one subject. Of his poems, only one or two can be said to be true letters. Poem 17 invites Ommatius, *vir clarissimus*, to a sixteenth birthday party. Having no doubt noticed that Horace, in inviting a friend, refrained from specifying a date in verse, he begins:

> quattuor ante dies quam lux Sextilis adusti
> prima spiciferum proferat orbe caput . . .

> (Four days before parched August's opening day
> Reveals on earth its corn-producing head . . .)

In Poem 12 Sidonius complains in hendecasyllables to Catullinus that he cannot, surrounded as he is by barbarians, write a poem on Venus. This is partly in the tradition of Ovid, penning his laments from the Black Sea, and partly of Statius, *Silv.*, IV.9, taunting Grypus for sending him a book gnawed by bookworms and crumbling with decay in return for his beautiful new book.

Horace's mould

Clearly the verse letter never established itself as a major genre. On the one hand, it could not compete with the lofty style of lyric, even though its length and subject-matter were often similar. On the other hand, the skilled composer had to avoid being excessively prosaic, and hence to avoid features too typical of the prose letter. Thus the epistolary imperfect, which we find so commonly used at the beginnings and ends of Cicero's letters, occurs once only in Horace.[17]

If we want to try to classify the main themes of Horace's letters, we shall find three: philosophy, literary criticism and auto-biography. Two, or all three of these, are from time to time inter-twined. Thus Homer (*Epist.*, 1.2) is praised as a moral teacher, while the philosophy of the right life, as in *Epist.*, 1.16 and 18, is coupled with Horace's enjoyment of the Sabine farm and its surroundings. Similarly his literary patronage (*Epist.*, 1.7) is bound up with the need he feels for a holiday.

In philosophic outlook Horace is undoubtedly an eclectic, though one with Epicurean leanings. He tells us plainly of his eclecticism in *Epist.*, 1.1.13-15:

> ac ne forte roges quo me duce, quo lare tuter,
> nullius addictus iurare in verba magistri,
> quo me cumque rapit tempestas, deferor hospes.

> (And just in case you ask who is my leader,
> Which is my tutelary deity,
> There is no master who has my allegiance;
> Wherever storms blow me, I land as guest.)

He goes on to explain that at one moment he feels like a stern Stoic, at the next like a happy hedonist of Aristippus' school. This is later cleverly borne out by his text, since *Epist.*, 1.16 ends with approval of Stoic suicide, while the very next letter has three mentions of Aristippus. As to the Epicureanism, that comes out, not only in the jocular allusion to a pig from Epicurus' sty (p. 100), but in the recommendation of a quiet life of contemplation in *Epist.*, 1.17.10, 1.18.97.

It has recently been argued[18] that Horace was far more indebted to Panaetius than is generally admitted. Panaetius of Rhodes, who taught and wrote in the second century B.C., was head of the Stoa from 129 to 109; but he was a somewhat unorthodox Stoic, incorporating ideas from Aristotle and others. Cicero modelled the first two books of his *De Officiis* largely on the work of Panaetius on duty. Certainly Horace's *decens*, 'what is fitting', corresponds to Panaetius' τὸ πρέπον. But some of the other equivalents suggested do not seem so certain; and parallels between Cicero's work and the Epistles are few.

As an eclectic Horace could, like the Stoic Seneca, have devoted all his epistles to philosophical themes only briefly introduced by topical allusions. But he has a different approach, influenced by what Heinze called 'Persönlichkeitsgefühl'.[19] Thus *Epist.*, 1.6 begins with the adage, associated with many shades of Greek philosophy, *nil admirari*, 'wonder at nothing', to which Shelley took such exception. But it goes on to a whole host of varied specific examples: the riches of the sea, the games in Rome, appreciation of works of art, the constant rat-race, a medical parallel, the king of Cappadocia rich only in slaves, Lucullus and his cache of cloaks, canvassing techniques, Gargilius' mock-hunt, the permissive attitude of Ulysses' crew. If this illustrative technique detracts from the course of pure philosophical inquiry, it at least enlivens the poems and relates them to contemporary life in Augustus' Rome and Italy.

There are many of Horace's letters which are concerned to a greater or lesser degree with literary criticism. Of these, the Letter to Florus (II.2) has a slight autobiographical background and devotes its last third to Horace's recent[20] preoccupation with ethics, introduced by a sentence (II.2.141–4) which sums up his programme as outlined in the first epistle of the first book:

> nimirum sapere est abiectis utile nugis,
> et tempestivum pueris concedere ludum,
> ac non verba sequi fidibus modulanda Latinis,[21]
> sed verae numerosque modosque ediscere vitae.

> (It surely helps to learn philosophy,
> Discarding trifles, and to leave to boys
> A game which suits their age; not to hunt out
> Words to be fitted to the Roman lyre,
> But learn a true life's rhythms and harmonies.)

Yet though the lyric form of the *Odes* was to be set aside, much of the verbal technique which Horace had acquired in composing the *Odes* remained. It is this which raises the *Epistles* to a higher level of composition, on the whole, than the *Satires*. Thus the light-hearted Lalage ending of the *integer vitae* ode (*Odes*, 1.22) perhaps inspires the jocular endings of *Epist.*, 1.1 and 1.4:

> ad summam, sapiens uno minor est Iove, dives,
> liber, honoratus, pulcher, rex denique regum,
> praecipue sanus, nisi cum pituita molesta est.

> (Well then, the wise man's only less than Jove:
> He's rich, free, honoured, handsome, king of kings,
> Above all, sound – unless he has a cold.)

> me pinguem et nitidum bene curata cute vises,
> cum ridere voles, Epicuri de grege porcum.

> (You want to have a laugh?
> Then visit me, sunburnt and fat and sleek,
> In fact a pig from Epicurus' sty.)[22]

This last is the end of the short letter to Albius, obviously the poet Tibullus, whose leg Horace must have been pulling when he asked if his friend was writing something to outdo the *opuscula* ('little works') of Cassius of Parma. Porphyrio and Pseudo-Acro were probably right in thinking that this Cassius is the same as the writer in *Sat.*, 1.10.61–4, who wrote so much that he was burnt to death by his own volumes. We should note that the alternative question as a syntactical construction (this forms the second half) is found also in the introductory sections of *Epist.*, 1.3, 1.11 and 1.16. In fact there is a stylistic parallelism between the third and fourth letters: (a) in each, line 1 opens with the vocative of the addressee; (b) in each, line 4 opens with *an* and has as its fourth word *inter*; (c) among the lines of each which are end-stopped are 2, 5, 7, 11 and 14.

The most serious letters dealing with literature are *Epist.*, 1.19, to Maecenas, and II.1, to Augustus. The letter to Maecenas is in effect a defence of *Odes*, I–III against two contradictory tendencies which Horace has observed since publication, namely servile imitation and hostile criticism. The letter is analysed by Fraenkel,[23] but there is one feature not discussed by him: the end of the poem surely reflects the poet's strong dislike of *recitationes*, which he considered in their prevalent form not so much readings of literature as mutual admiration societies. One of the chief promoters of these reading salons was C. Asinius Pollio, whose histories he had praised in *Odes*, II.1 but whose enthusiasm for *recitationes* he could not share.[24] If Pollio, noted for the severity of his criticisms,[25] had despite that flattering passage been among those who found fault with certain aspects of Horace's published odes, this might explain the rather catty phrase in l. 39, *nobilium scriptorum auditor et ultor*, which Horace says he is not, 'one who listens to well-known writers and takes his revenge on them'.

The autobiographical element comes out most strongly in *Epist.*, 1.20, where the poet describes his appearance in much detail, as short, greying in front, fond of sunbathing, easily losing his temper but only for a short time. Other letters too, such as 1.4 quoted above, supplemented by Augustus' correspondence (p. 95), fill out the picture. Horace on the Sabine farm struggling to move clods of earth, Horace the traveller choosy about his wines, Horace relaxing in country or seaside, these and many other sketches emerge from the letters. In *Epist.*, II.2.65 ff. he

gives a frantic picture of life in Rome. He has to visit one man on
the Quirinal on legal business, another on the Aventine to listen
to his writings (72–5):

> festinat calidus mulis gerulisque redemptor,[26]
> torquet nunc lapidem, nunc ingens machina tignum,
> tristia robustis luctantur funera plaustris,
> hac rabiosa fugit canis, hac lutulenta ruit sus.

> (A builder dashes by with mules and porters;
> A giant crane is moving blocks and beams.
> Sad funeral hearses jostle sturdy carts;
> Here a mad dog runs, there a filthy pig.)

Traffic and pollution may not have reached their present formidable proportions in Rome, but the poet could well despair of
composing melodious verses in such surroundings. This throws
light on his insistence in *Epist.*, 1.7 on staying at the Sabine farm
rather than going to Rome in the heat of the summer, and even
after; but he puts it so tactfully that Wieland (1782) was clearly
over-stressing the threatened break in relationships between
Maecenas and Horace.[27]

It is clear that in at least some cases the poet carefully adapted
his language to the interests and background of his addressee. An
example of this is *Epist.*, 1.5, written to the lawyer, Torquatus.
There must be some allusion, hidden to us, in *Archiacis . . . lectis*
(l. 1), the couches to which Torquatus is asked to accommodate
himself in the poet's triclinium. Might they indeed, as Porphyrio
suggests, be very short couches? In that case Torquatus may have
been the opposite of Horace, a very tall man, as his presumably
patrician birth (cf. *Odes*, IV.7) and warrior ancestry might make
more likely. Why stress the vintage of Taurus' second consulship,
26 B.C.? Perhaps not only a good year but one memorable in
Torquatus' career. Why a wine from the area between Minturnae
and the Mons Petrinus? Probably, as suggested by R. G. M.
Nisbet,[28] to allude to a battle fought by the lawyer's famous
ancestor, T. Manlius Torquatus. Why does Horace say he 'orders
himself' (*imperor*, l. 21) to see that all is well for the meal? Perhaps,
as likewise suggested by Nisbet, an allusion to the *imperia
Manliana*, the severe order from T. Manlius that his son should be
put to death for disobedience on the field of battle. Why such a

series of *ne* clauses following? Possibly to imitate the language of legal documents. We may conclude with Gordon Williams that the setting is implausible and the invitation hardly a genuine one.

We must also admire the skilled use of dialogue by Horace, a form inherited from Plato[29] and from the diatribe and other popular philosophy of the Hellenistic Age. In *Epist.*, 1.7.15–19 we see a typical example: Maecenas has not, in enriching Horace, acted like the Calabrian host with his pears. We note how each of the host's sentences increases in number of words as it decreases in politeness.

> 'vescere sodes.'
> 'iam satis est.' 'at tu quantum vis tolle.' 'benigne.'
> 'non invisa feres pueris munuscula parvis.'
> 'tam teneor dono quam si dimittar onustus.'
> 'ut libet; haec porcis hodie comedenda relinques.'

> ('Please eat some.' 'That's enough.' 'No, take away
> As many as you like.' 'Many thanks, no.'
> 'They'll make a lovely present for the children.'
> 'Your offer is as welcome as a load.'
> 'Just as you like. The pigs will eat them up.')

These lines are followed by two couplets in which the stupid man who palms off useless gifts (*prodigus et stultus*) is contrasted with the good, wise man (*vir bonus et sapiens*), of whom Maecenas is the prototype. The parallelism of form emphasizes the contrast of personalities.

But in looking at the *Odes* for parallels and in tracing the *Epistles* back to their probable literary antecedents, we must not forget the recurring debt to Lucilius and to Horace's own *Satires*.[30] This debt is present throughout, both in content and in form. It is, for example, almost certainly to be seen in a number of the men's names introduced into the text. Whereas the addressees are contemporaries, these names look like importations from Lucilius familiar to the learned reader. We know that Maenius, the spendthrift of *Epist.*, 1.15.26 ff., was a Lucilian character. But not content with importing Maenius, who had already made an appearance in *Sat.*, 1.3.21–3, Horace tells us (*Epist.*, 1.15.37) that Maenius behaved like a reformed Bestius: who Bestius was we do not know, but the bulk of Horace's readers must have, and he

may well have been another Lucilian character. We know that
Gallonius (*Sat.*, II.2.47) came from Lucilius, so it is likely that
Gargilius (*Epist.*, 1.6.56–61), who took hunting equipment to the
forum to pretend he had hunted a boar which he really bought,
and Gargonius,[31] who had 'B.O.' (*Sat.*, 1.2.27; 1.4.92), also did. In
Epist., 1.1.74–5 Horace refers to the fable of the fox and the lion[32]
when asked why he does not bow to popular judgment, continuing:

> referam: 'quia me vestigia terrent
> omnia te adversum spectantia, nulla retrorsum.'

(I shall reply: 'Because the tracks alarm me;
All of them face towards you, none face back.')

Lucilius has the lines:[33]

> quid sibi vult, qua re fit ut introvorsus et ad te
> spectent atque ferant vestigia se omnia prorsus?

(What means it or how comes it that the tracks
Face inwards and towards you, looking your way?)

The words *vestigia, omnia, te, spectare* have been retained, but
duplication has twice been avoided and the point made clearer in
fewer words. The reference to drunken Pyrr(h)ia (*Epist.*, 1.13.14),
if that is the correct form of the name,[34] carrying a ball of stolen
wool, would be much more intelligible to Horace's readers if it
came through the medium of Lucilius than if he drew it direct
from the comic writer, Titinius.

Although Horace did not make a boastful claim about the
future of this genre which he had done much to perfect, such as he
had in *Odes*, III.30 about the first three books of *Odes*, he did fore-
see a role for his first book of *Epistles*, among other uses as a
schoolbook. (Hence the witty epilogue with language which
would equally well suit a book or a youth selling his favours.) He
had always seen himself as a teacher: 'it is to girls and boys that I
sing' (*Odes*, III.1.4). In his search for the right life, what appealed
to him was the children's song:

> rex eris si recte facies; si non facies, non eris.

(Do the right thing,
You'll be a king.
If you don't,
Then you won't.)

The addressee of the second and eighteenth epistles, Lollius
Maximus, was at the time of the second epistle a boy: Fairclough
calls him a young man, but Horace's word is *puer*, and declamation
was for boys as well as young men.[35] He is the only recipient of
more than one letter in the first book apart from Maecenas. It
need not surprise us that Horace addressed his letter on the Art of
Poetry to the two young Pisos rather than to an adult or the reader
at large.

Some lines of Horace's *Epistles* were applied to the theory of
education by a medieval writer. Among the Horatian passages
quoted by John of Salisbury, Bishop of Chartres, is one (*Meta-
logicon*, 1.7) from *Epist.*, 1.4.7–11, where Horace has said that the
gods had given Albius (Tibullus) beauty, wealth and the art of
enjoying it:

> quid voveat dulci nutricula maius alumno,
> qui sapere et fari possit quae sentiat, et cui
> gratia, fama, valetudo contingat abunde,
> et mundus victus non deficiente crumina?

> (Would a fond nurse pray for a greater gift
> Than these for her dear boy, if wisdom, speech
> To utter feelings, popularity,
> Fame and good health came copiously, as also
> A decent living and an ample purse?)

John comments that our poet has his priorities right: (1) philosophy, to the mind of each the most important study (the bishop's
advocacy, as James J. Murphy has observed, may have had a profound effect on the development of universities); (2) rhetoric,
since all should also learn to be eloquent; (3) the qualities admired
by the world; (4) enough money. The *ethicus*, as John of Salisbury
names him, did not know that his word order as well as his obiter
dicta would be important 1,200 years later.

Horace and numbers

Although our poet was called by Ovid *numerosus*,[36] that does not
mean 'fond of numbers' but 'good at rhythm'. This he certainly
was, and perhaps musical too;[37] the question is to what extent he
thought numerically. Patterns within sections of his odes have

been analysed;[38] some of these undoubtedly show a preoccupation with symmetry and proportion. A more sweeping statement is made by G. Stégen,[39] who claims that many of the epistles are divided into two halves, four quarters and so on: 'De là, selon l'importance de l'épître, on peut aller à 16 et même à 32 sub-divisions . . . Une certaine latitude est en effet laissée dans les nombres, mais jamais on ne perd de vue les subdivisions fonda-mentales: 100, 50, 25, 12, 6, 3.' He gives as an example *Epist.*, 1.1, where he says that the first 93 lines, which constitute a whole, can be divided into halves, quarters, eighths and so on down to sixty-fourths (ll. 16–17, 18–19). This theory cannot be substanti-ated. From the mathematical angle we may observe that groups of three lines cannot be called thirty-seconds if groups of two lines are called sixty-fourths; and that 93 is too far from his figure to lend any weight to his theory. Certainly the epistle has ll. 3, 6, 9, 12 and 15 each closing a sentence, and the last three lines also form one. But if we go further, we shall find ourselves looking for patterns where none exists.

This does not mean, however, that Horace is unaware of the importance of precision. One who advocated publishing no poetry for eight years after it was written was likely to be precise. But the precision of the hexameter works is of a somewhat differ-ent nature, which may conveniently be examined in the twenty letters of the first book.

If we detach *Epist.*, 1.20 as an epilogue addressed to his book, there are nineteen others, of which the first two and last two are thus addressed: 1.1 to Maecenas; 1.2 to Lollius Maximus; 1.18 to Lollius (obviously the same); 1.19 to Maecenas. *Epist.*, 1.1 starts *prima dicte mihi, summa dicende Camena*, 'first invoked by me, last to be invoked', and this is true not only in broader terms,[40] but of these nineteen letters too. *Camena* in 1.1.1 is matched by *Camenae*, 1.19.5. *Epist.*, 1.1 and 1.19 review Horace's position after the pub-lication of *Odes* I–III, (a) from the philosophical, (b) from the literary point of view. Three-quarters of the way through each, *Epist.*, 1.1.70 ff. and 1.19.35 ff., he defends his refusal to court popularity. In the opening of *Epist.*, 1.1 and in the end of *Epist.*, 1.19 he has metaphors from gladiatorial fights and wrestling respectively, with the word *ludus* playing a prominent part in each.

A comparative analysis of 1.2 and 1.18 has been made by

Fraenkel. [41] Contrary to the pair just mentioned, this pair has the literature (Homer) before the philosophy. Horace's love of the Golden Mean comes out in each, especially in 1.18.9, the Aristotelian maxim:

> virtus est medium vitiorum et utrimque reductum

> (Goodness is equally removed from vices
> On either side.)

Similarly at the end of 1.2 the poet says he will neither wait if Lollius is slow nor strain himself to catch up with racers. Each of the two letters has the vocative *Lolli* at the end of the first line: but more important, each deals with the correct use of speech, the control of the emotions, the importance of a balanced mind. A line in the second half of each, 1.2.43 and 1.18.71, has a wonderful accommodation of sound to sense.

The connection of thought between other pairs in the ring composition may be as follows: (a) 1.3 and 1.17, getting on with the great (this is uncertain, as the advice to Florus makes it clear that he had failed to get on with Munatius, but does not discuss relations with Tiberius); (b) 1.4 and 1.16, the effect of life in the country on Tibullus and Horace respectively; (c) 1.5 and 1.15, eating and drinking; (d) 1.6 and 1.14, is either the rich man's or the poor man's ideal of life in Rome really enviable? (e) 1.7 and 1.13, Horace's relations with Maecenas and with Augustus; (f) 1.8 and 1.12, two letters to (or for) men working for those closest to Augustus; both contain medical metaphors; (g) 1.9 and 1.11, here the connection, if present, seems to be allusion. Septimius of 1.9 is no doubt the same as the friend of *Odes*, ii.6, who would go with the poet to the west of Spain, but who is told that Horace intends to end his days at Tibur or Tarentum; in *Epist.*, 1.11 the poet rejects Lebedos in Asia Minor as a place of retirement. This leaves only 1.10, and as that is placed centrally, it is no doubt intentionally divided into two equal halves – ll. 1–25 the contrasting claims of city and country; ll. 26–50 (including ll. 49–50 epilogue), the ethical implications of these.

Apart from ring composition, it is possible to trace connections of thought between one epistle and the next. For example, 1.6 and 1.7 both deal, in different ways, with the bustle and rat-race of Rome. Sometimes the connection is more partial, e.g. 1.7.86–7 and 1.8.4–6 both deal with agricultural problems. Sometimes it lies in single words, and here in at least one case we can discern something of a mathematical pattern. One of the most prominent words in the *Epistles* is *vivere*, often in the connotation of living rightly. If we turn to *Epist.*, 1.10, 1.11 and 1.12, we find the following occurrences of this verb: *Epist.*, 1.10: ll. 8, 12, 44; *Epist.*, 1.11: ll. 8, 12, 24, 29; *Epist.*, 1.12: l. 8 (*bis*). There is surely more than mere coincidence in these line numbers.

An effect of this sort makes one wonder whether the *Ars Poetica* was not deliberately divided, as has been thought,[42] into ll. 1–294 and 295–476, so as to produce two totals each divisible by 14,[43] giving the proportion 21:34. These are consecutive numbers in the Fibonacci series, on which the so-called Golden Mean is based. Although it is only one example, it can at least be considered more clear-cut than most of the examples which G. E. Duckworth[44] has claimed for the *Aeneid*. But Horace uses art to conceal art. In order to bridge the gap he has two references to finger-nails, *non castigavit ad unguem* immediately before it and *bona pars non ungues ponere curat* in the sentence immediately following it (*Ars Poetica*, 294, 297). We do not find this effect in his other works. Thus in the *Odes* the most noticeable effect seems to be a stress on the central portion of quite a number of poems,[45] e.g. *Odes*, 1.9, 11.10, 11.15, 111.1, 111.4, 111.16, 111.29. The central phrases are not infrequently connected with Horace's view of life, which aimed at the happy medium. From the point of view of symmetry it has been pointed out that the group of twelve odes, which open Book 11 and are marked among other things by the alternation of alcaics and sapphics in eleven of them, has twenty-eight of the original odes before it and twenty-eight after it.

Finally, we may perhaps indulge in a more fanciful speculation. In the first book of *Epistles* Horace merely complains of advancing years and gives his age in 20 B.C. as forty-four (*Epist.*, 1.20.27–8). He several times advises others against investigating the future. But in *Odes*, 11.17 he prophesies that Maecenas and he will die at the same time, whenever Maecenas leads the way. We are told that in 8 B.C. Maecenas died, commending his protégé to Augustus in his will, and that a month or two later Horace too died. But did Horace also have an actual vision of his age at death? Although we can never tell this, it is at least curious that *Odes*, 1.11, the poem in which he tells Leuconoe not to inquire what end the gods have appointed for him or her, not to attempt Babylonian (astrological) numbers, contains fifty-six words. Horace was fifty-six years old (nearly fifty-seven) when he died. Could he have written this poem with a premonition of that number?[46] A modern parallel may perhaps be seen in Lorca's poem 'Fabula y Rueda de los Tres Amigos',[47] where the poet imagines himself assassinated and sought in vain: 'comprendí que me habían asesinado . . . Ya no me encontraron . . .' To interpret such a statement allegorically seems somehow to miss the point, when we know that Lorca was in fact assassinated and his body was not found.

Horace's allegory was of partial survival, *non omnis moriar*, 'not all of me will die' (*Odes*, III.30.6). He would have been gratified, 2,000 years after,[48] to see (not that the words directly allude to this) that all his poetry survived. And if some had to be selected, many of us would like to choose that part of his work in which, as has most justly been said, he 'is most completely like himself'.[49]

Notes

1 *Odes*, IV.3.23, *Romanae fidicen lyrae*; cf. *Epist.*, I.19.32 ff., *Latinus . . . fidicen*; II.2.143, quoted on p. 100; Ovid, *Tristia*, IV.10.49, of Horace, *dum ferit Ausonia carmina culta lyra*. For a criticism of the implication that there is no shift of attitude between the first two passages quoted above, see G. Williams's review of C. O. Brink's book, *Prolegomena to the Literary Epistles* (Cambridge, 1963), 'Horace on poetry', *JRS*, 54 (1964), 186–96.

2 The fullest treatment is in H. Peter, *Der Brief in der römischen Litteratur*, Leipzig, 1901.

3 Translation by G. R. Morrow, 1962. The first letter is spurious; the remainder may well be by Plato.

4 *De Elocutione*, 223, trans. G. M. A. Grube, *A Greek Critic: Demetrius on Style* (Phoenix Suppl. vol. iv), Toronto, 1961.

5 G. Giangrande, *The Use of Spoudaiogeloion in Greek and Roman Literature* (Studies in Classical Literature, 6), The Hague, 1971.

6 *Ad fam.*, II.4.1. For a recent biography of Cicero based mainly on his extant letters see D. R. Shackleton Bailey, *Cicero*, London, 1971.

7 Nepos, *Atticus*, 20.2, says that Augustus kept up a voluminous correspondence with Atticus, consulting him sometimes on antiquities, sometimes on a point of poetry, while at times by joking he elicited more wordy letters from Atticus.

8 Life of Horace attributed to Suetonius: 'itaque licebit in sextariolo scribas, quo circuitus voluminis tui sit ὀγκωδέστερος (MS. reading – τατος), sicut est ventriculi tui.' See E. Fraenkel, *Horace*, Oxford, 1957, pp. 20–1 and notes.

9 Cicero, *Ad Att.*, XIII.6a (=6.4); *Brut.*, 94.

10 Lucilius, ed. Marx (1905), 181–8; ed. Warmington, *Remains of Old Latin*, III, Loeb, 186–93.

11 The description so aptly fits the rather large villa near the Digentia (Licenza) that one should have no hesitation in making the identification; see G. Lugli, *Horace's Sabine Farm*, 1930. Since we know that the farm was worked by eight slaves (*Sat.*, II.7.118), we can discount the impression of semi-poverty left us by Horace's other writings. For this letter see M. J. McGann, 'The sixteenth epistle of Horace', *CQ*, n.s., 10 (1960), 205 ff.; C. Becker, *Das Spätwerk des Horaz*, Göttingen, 1963, pp. 17–19.

12 Ps.–Acro is probably right in attributing ll.7–10 to Bullatius.

13 The original title was perhaps *Epistulae Heroidum*.

14 The word *silvae*, like 'anthology' and other such names, is merely a title, drawn from nature, for a collection of poems. See Gellius, *praef.*, 5 ff.; Statius, *Silvae*, vol. 1, ed. H. Frère (Budé edn, Paris, 1944), pp. xxxii – xxxiv.

15 The poem, which contains the customary rhetorical ornament and is to some extent based on the *suasoria*, seems nevertheless to represent Statius' thoughts on a genuine family crisis.

16 A good way of examining Pliny's editing methods is to compare Pliny, *Ep.*, III.21 with Martial, x.19: Pliny has excerpted from Martial's poem what suits him and nothing more. Thus his house in Rome must not be described as 'Pedo's little house': he presumably regarded himself as a greater literary figure than Albinovanus Pedo had been.

17 *Epist.*, I.10.49. When Horace wishes to put *vale* near the end of a letter, he couples it with another imperative: *Epist.*, I.6.67; I.13.19 (could this be a pun on Vinnius' presumed cognomen, for which see n. 28 below?). In *Epist.*, I.7.3, 'si me vivere vis sanum recteque valentem', we may have an echo of the traditional opening formula, 'si vales, bene est; ego quoque valeo'.

18 M. J. McGann, *Studies in Horace's First Book of Epistles* (Collection Latomus, vol. C), Brussels, 1969.

19 W. S. Maguinness, 'Friendship and the philosophy of friendship in Horace', *Hermathena*, 51 (1938), 29–48, stresses the friendship aspect of Horace's philosophical beliefs.

20 The epistle to Florus probably dates to 19 B.C.; see C. Becker, *Das Spätwerk des Horaz*, pp. 61–2.

21 Cf. the passages quoted in n. 1 above.

22 Either for metrical reasons or as too derogatory, Horace avoids the word *hara*, 'sty': Cicero, *Pis.*, 37, 'Epicure noster ex hara producte non ex schola . . .'

23 Op. cit., pp. 314–21.

24 *Sat.* 1.4.73, 'nec recito cuiquam nisi amicis, idque coactus'.

25 It was he who referred to Livy's *Patavinitas* and deplored archaisms in Sallust.

26 Cf. *Odes*, III.1.35, of the contractor and his employees building out a rich man's house over the sea; *Epist.*, I.1.83 ff. for Horace's attitude to this in the *Epistles*.

27 See C. Becker, *Das Spätwerk des Horaz*, pp. 25–37, with bibliography in notes 5 and 6; E. Fraenkel, *Horace*, pp. 327–39; M. J. McGann, *Studies in Horace's First Book of Epistles*, pp. 48–56.

28 R. G. M. Nisbet, 'Notes on Horace, *Epistles* I', *CQ*, n.s., 9 (1959), 73–6; G. Williams. *Tradition and Originality in Roman Poetry*, Oxford, 1968, pp. 7–10; F. Cairns, *Generic Composition in Greek and Roman Poetry*, Edinburgh, 1972, pp. 241–2. There is also no doubt in the present writer's mind that Nisbet is correct in identifying the Vinnius of *Epist.*, 1.13 with Vinnius Valens, centurion of the praetorian guard, a man of outstanding strength: hence the joke about the heavy burden of carrying a few writings of Horace's. See also n. 17 above.

29 Orelli may have been right in thinking that the Plato packed by Horace for country reading along with Menander, Eupolis and Archilochus (*Sat.*, II.3.11–12) was the philosopher, not the comic poet. We still get an 'odd man out' even if we think of three comic poets. In *A.P.*, 310, Horace has the sentence 'rem tibi Socraticae poterunt ostendere chartae': subject-matter for the dramatist will, he says, be revealed in the form of moral principles, of which 'Socratic' writings are the source recommended. C. O. Brink, *Horace on Poetry: the 'Ars Poetica'*, Cambridge, 1971, p. 388, says: ' "Books of moral philosophy" may be all that is in mind'; but Horace may have been thinking particularly of Plato's Socratic dialogues.

30 See N. Rudd, *The Satires of Horace*, Cambridge, 1966.

31 For Gargonius see also Seneca, *Epist.*, 86. 13.

32 The parallel is commented on by Rudd, op. cit., pp. 100 f.

33 Marx, op. cit., 988–9; Warmington, op. cit., 1119–20.

34 It should by analogy be a male name, Pyrrhias. For the style of this passage see L. P. Wilkinson, *Golden Latin Artistry*, Cambridge, 1966, p. 201.

35 Thus Seneca, *Contr.*, 1.1.22, writes of a boy prodigy, Alfius Flavus, who attracted crowds by his declamation.

36 *Tristia*, IV. 10.48 f. Ovid clearly enjoyed listening to Horace.

37 This is the theory of N. A. Bonavia-Hunt, *Horace the Minstrel*, London, 1954. It cannot be disproved, but ancient poets are fond of describing their poetry in musical terms.

38 N. E. Collinge, *The Structure of Horace's Odes* (University of Durham Publications), London, 1961.

39 *L'unité et la clarté des Epîtres d'Horace; étude sur sept pièces du premier livre* (*4, 6, 7, 9, 13, 14, 16*), Namur, 1963, p. 5, referring also to his *Essai sur la composition de cinq Epîtres d'Horace* (*I, 1, 2, 3, 11, 15*), Namur, 1960.

40 It has been observed that towards the end of his period of composition Horace does not address poems so assiduously to Maecenas; but this may not indicate any cooling off in their relations.

41 Op. cit., pp. 314–21.

42 K. Gantar, 'De compositione Horatii "Epistulae ad Pisones" ', *ZAnt*, 4 (1954), 277. The line totals given assume that there is no lacuna and that no lines in the MSS. should be deleted, whereas C. O. Brink, *Horace on*

Poetry: the 'Ars Poetica', postulates a lacuna of one line after 61 and considers 349 spurious.

43 Whereas 7 is a magic number, there is no reason why 14 should have been chosen in particular; it is merely a question of suitable length.

44 *Structural Patterns and Proportions in Vergil's Aeneid*, University of Michigan, 1962.

45 L. A. Moritz, 'Some "central" thoughts on Horace's Odes', *CQ*, n.s., 18 (1968), 116–31.

46 R. G. M. Nisbet and Margaret Hubbard, in their edition of Horace, *Odes*, I, Oxford, 1970, pp. 134–42, consider that Horace, as a follower of Epicurus, refused to have anything to do with clairvoyance, whereas not only Leuconoe but Maecenas himself had evidently dabbled in it.

47 F. García Lorca, *Poeta en Nueva York*, Mexico, 1940; cf. Lorca, selected and translated by J. L. Gili, Harmondsworth, 1960, p. xi. For the information on Lorca I am indebted to Mr David Burnett of Grey College, Durham, and to correspondence which he had with the editor of the Penguin volume.

48 1972 was the 2000th anniversary of the decisive year 29 B.C., when Augustus celebrated his triple triumph and closed the temple of Janus, and when Horace was probably inspired to write his *Odes*.

49 J. A. K. Thomson, *The Classical Background of English Literature*, London, 1948, p. 86.

Ars Poetica

D. A. Russell

Quintilian[1] alludes to this poem as *ars poetica* or *liber de arte poetica*. The manuscript tradition, instead of associating it with the *Epistles*, gives it a separate place, in company with the *Odes* and *Epodes*. Its differences from the *Epistles* are in fact more significant for its understanding than its resemblances to them. It is very much 'a treatise with *Dear so-and-so* at the beginning'.[2] Its length, its didactic formulae, the recurrent addresses to the Pisones in the manner of Lucretius' to Memmius, and especially its very technical content, mark it out as an experiment. Perhaps it was the last of the great innovator's new creations; for, though the arguments about its date[3] are indecisive, there is much to be said for a late one, after the last book of the *Odes*. Porphyrio's identification of the Piso father with the future *praefectus urbi*[4] (48 B.C. – A.D. 32) may be right after all: he could well have had, by his late thirties, two sons old enough to be thought interested in poetry.

What Horace is attempting is, to put it as briefly as possible, a poem on poetics. Both halves of this description, however, need to be clarified. Despite *nil scribens ipse* (306), where Horace speaks as the non-practising theorist, the *Ars*, like the *Epistles* and *Satires*, is composed on poetical principles. Transitions and movements of thought depend on verbal association and emotional tone rather than on logical or rhetorical arrangement. The choice of topics and the degree of elaboration accorded to them is determined, as in Lucretius or the *Georgics*, more by the poetical potential or viability of the theme than by the need to give a certain weight to a certain matter because of its place in an overall pattern of argument or precept. Second, the subject of this eccentric didactic poem – as far removed from the norm of the *Georgics* as Ovid's *Ars* was to be – is not poetry, but poetics: the body of theory formulated, largely out of earlier insights, by Aristotle and his successors, and current in Hellenistic times in a variety of handbooks and summaries.

Porphyrio, of course, informs us that Horace drew specially on one such handbook:

> congessit praecepta Neoptolemi τοῦ Παριανοῦ de arte poetica, non quidem omnia sed eminentissima.

We naturally view this with scepticism, mindful of the exaggeration with which ancient scholarship was wont to proclaim discoveries of derivation and plagiarism. We do not believe Servius when he tells us that *Aeneid* IV comes *paene totus* from Apollonius' *Argonautica*, because we can check the facts. Why then should we believe Porphyrio here? A fair analogy; but even Servius does not lie, he only exaggerates. Porphyrio should be given the credit of a right, or at least plausible, diagnosis. What little we know in other ways of Neoptolemus supports the case. But suppose we had Neoptolemus *in extenso*: is it likely that this would further our understanding of the *Ars* more than, say, Varro's *De re rustica* furthers our understanding of the *Georgics*?[5] The poem before us does not after all look at all like a versified treatise. Nor, on all the analogies that ancient literature affords, was it written to make poets of us or the Pisones. Its aim surely was to please us and compliment them.

Yet (l. 343)

> Omne tulit punctum qui miscuit utile dulci.

Is not Horace trying to do this too? Of course; but in a way that needs defining. Peripatetic treatises on poetics tended to have a certain layout, resting on general theory: basically, it would seem, the principle of Aristotle's *Rhetoric* (not to be found in the *Poetics*) that content and argument should be discussed independently of form and language. This simple division into 'what is to be said' and 'how it is to be said' goes back anyway to Plato, for we find it in the moral critique of poetry which he makes in *Republic* II and III.[6] It exists in more sophisticated forms in the Hellenistic critics: the famous ποίημα/ποίησις distinction in Neoptolemus is one of these, for ποίησις (the act of composing a whole poem) deals with the entire business of plot, and ποίημα (the work of making verses, or the verses so made) involves the entire topic of the linguistic medium.[7] Now Horace does indeed recognize this res/verba division (40 ff.). And he naturally discusses vocabulary at some length in some places, and plot at some length in others. But he does not submit his exposition to it as a principle of division of the material, as a textbook writer would. Even if one supposes (and there is plausibility in this) a shift from form to content at l. 118, it is heavily overlaid: simplicity and variety, with which the poem begins, are topics of content; vocabulary and metre, matters of form, recur often enough in the latter part, from l. 232 onwards. The most significant point of technical arrangement in the poem is the simple one, often observed, that the whole of the last part (from about l. 295) is devoted, not to the poet's works, but to his person and function in society. The caricature at the end is of the mad, disorganized poet; the caricature at the beginning, which it seems to balance, is of the chaotic, disorganized work of art. Now we know that Philodemus criticized in Neoptolemus the tripartite division of the subject ποίημα/ποίησις/ποιητής.[8] It is an obvious and captious point, not untypical of much ancient polemic, that a poet is not a species of poetry. But however unfair Philodemus' argument, we need scarcely doubt that this is how Neoptolemus divided the matter. In following him, Horace not only reproduced a textbook order of things, but (far more important) opened his own way to satire and moral interest.

I shall return to this point. In all other respects, the process of turning poetics into poetry manifestly did not depend on a given articulation of the subject. What was far more important to Horace was the richness of the topics built into the system. These we may group in two sets of three. The first set consists of certain ideas which were of basic importance in Aristotelian theory and its Hellenistic developments: unity, propriety (decorum), the historical development of the genres and in particular of drama. The second comprises themes to which Horace seems to have devoted more space than we might have expected: the importance of ars compared with ingenium – a presupposition of anyone who writes an ars;[9] the commitment of the poet not only to conscientious workmanship but to socially valuable moral principles; and the difference between Roman attitudes and Greek. These latter points arise mainly in the last part of the poem; they represent the most serious lesson it has to teach. For towards the end the 'poem on poetics' seems to become more hortatory. It is not indeed a protreptic to poetry. The Pisones might well find it rather a warning off (372–3):

> Mediocribus esse poetis
> non homines, non di, non concessere columnae.

It is difficult to write a sentence about the *Ars*, especially one which claims to paraphrase it, without acute diffidence. Problems posed, solved or dissolved by four centuries of scholarship have resulted in a neurotic confusion unexcelled even in classical studies. It is easy to see how this has happened. Here is a poem the content of which has seemed peculiarly important in every age when European literature has looked back to its classical roots. It is also a poem of great delicacy and allusiveness. There is a sort of printing in two tones which reveals different legends as you turn it towards or away from the light. A lot of the *Ars* is like that. Lines and sections read quite differently according to what you hold in mind from the context, and whether you look forwards or back. Analysis is therefore almost always controversial. Anyone who undertakes to guide a party round the poem is likely to be pointing out things that are not there, and missing things that are. Nevertheless, some sort of paraphrase is the only help worth having. So I attempt one.

'While he teacheth the art, he goeth unartificially to work, even in the very beginning'[10] wrote a seventeenth-century critic, following Scaliger's damning phrase, *ars sine arte tradita*. But the caricature of the Scylla-like monster with which the poem opens is in fact not without art. An introductory comparison, often quite bizarre, is a common exordium, for example, in works of popular philosophy like Plutarch's. It attracts attention, and relates the subject to something outside it – a good move to excite interest. Here, by relating poetry to painting, Horace makes a special point: both are forms of imitation, traditionally paired together. Painting, said Simonides, is silent poetry.[11]

When unity and disunity are in question, Horace thinks particularly of epic: so here, so also below in ll. 136–52. A grand enterprise is spoilt by a superfluous description (*ecphrasis*), however pretty it may be. A 'purple patch', in fact, involves a breach not only of unity but of *decorum*, since this implies the consistent maintenance of a single tone of discourse. But the main point in all this paragraph is unity: it is emphasized by two more parallels, from painting and pottery (19–22), and by the analogy of other literary vices.

These last lines (24–31) deserve a closer look. The general principle they convey is that the effort to achieve some good quality often leads us into a bad one: brevity into obscurity, smoothness into flabbiness, grandeur into bombast, caution into dullness – and variety into absurdity. This is standard literary theory, based ultimately on the Aristotelian doctrine of 'mean' and 'extremes'.[12] The way out of the danger is afforded by *ars*; this alone enables us to distinguish success from failure. Horace's economy is noteworthy: in a few lines, he reminds us of the traditional 'three styles' – grand, slight and smooth – as well of the traditional justification of *ars* and the relation of the question of unity to the more general one of technique. At the same time he elaborates on his theme with charm and humour: on the *ecphrasis* (17–19), on the unsuccessful sculptor in bronze (32–5), on beautiful black eyes and hair (37).

Alternation between fullness and brevity is a feature of the poem, one of its chief techniques of variety. This is perhaps to be regarded as a Hesiodic inheritance, for the *Works and Days*, a much-studied model for the Alexandrians, is like this: brief gnomic wisdom alternates with set pieces of description. Nowhere is this technique clearer than in the next part of the *Ars*. First, a fundamental *praeceptum*: choose your subject within your powers (38–40). This is elaborated only to the extent of being said twice over, with a certain amount of metaphor (*umeri*) and anaphora (*quid . . . quid . . .*). From competent choice of subject will follow both style and arrangement (40–1). These two are taken up in reverse order: arrangement of material briefly (42–5),[13] vocabulary at length. Characteristically Augustan is the emphasis laid on ingenious word-combination (*iunctura*, σύνθεσις) as the road to distinction and novelty. It could be a veiled compliment to Virgil, whose detractors turned this notion on its head to speak of the insidious affectation (*cacozelia*) inherent in his use of common words.[14] The theory of poetic vocabulary involved various topics: foreign words or 'glosses,' metaphors and neologisms. Horace chooses only the last. It has no doubt a special relevance to Latin, where the conscious expansion of vocabulary on Greek lines was an active issue. More important, it leads to a general topic with a moral aspect: the dependence of vocabulary on usage (*usus*) and the consequent mortality of words. The conventional exemplification of *debemur morti nos nostraque* (61) takes us for a while away from the critic's lecture to the world outside.

At l. 73 comes a sharp break. The entertaining survey of metres in relation to genres looks wholly forward, to the *discriptas . . . vices operumque colores* of l. 86. Metre is the principal differentia of genre. But ll. 86–8 seem at first sight to look both ways: not only back to the metres but on to ll. 89–98, to the differentiation of tragedy from comedy by language, and the circumstances in which each may sometimes usurp the other's manner. It is a question of some importance whether this apparent double face is really there. The passage on metre is incomplete without ll. 86–7. It is the same sort of economical incorporation of background theory that we saw in ll. 25–8, and like that passage is futile without its conclusion. On the other hand, the passage 89–98 has a completeness in itself. It does not need the generalization, though it may be held to illustrate it. We should, I think, be careful not to seek connections where they are not. Hesiod reminds us that chains of *gnomai* often have loose or broken links. A reading of the ancient technical treatises – notably Demetrius, *On Style* – should warn us further that even these works are often lacking in logical order. In interpreting this passage, we should allow for some deliberate disjointedness: paragraph not (as some editors) at l. 85, but at ll. 88, 91, 92, 98.

All this is about drama. Epic has slipped from sight, the other genres appear only incidentally as examples of the diverse *colores*. This concentration is typical of Peripatetic criticism. It becomes more and more pronounced as the *Ars* proceeds. From now on, the whole of the poem (up to l. 295) is concerned with drama, except for ll. 131–52, an encomium of Homer which is an evident digression. It is a natural and proper conclusion from this that the scope of the poem is something different from a critique of the contemporary Augustan literary scene. However important those lost masterpieces, Varius' *Thyestes* and Ovid's *Medea*, may have been, they were marginal to the Augustan achievement. Strange if Horace did not know this too. The literary scene, which is his subject for example in the *Letter to Augustus* (*Epist.*, II.1), is not the topic here: here it is the theory that he takes as his material.

Diction, said the textbooks,[15] should be appropriate to emotion, character and circumstance. Horace follows this pattern: emotion

(99–111), circumstance (112–13), character (114–18) – in the usual technical sense of the determinate *ēthos* of a particular sort of person. Much of the detail of this discussion is known to be part of the technical tradition. With ll. 114–17, we rightly compare the censure of Aristophanes in Plutarch:[16] 'You could not tell whether it is a son talking or a father or a farmer or a god or an old woman or a hero.' What remains puzzling is probably traditional also: the mysterious Colchian, Assyrian, Theban and Argive (118) will also have a history in lost books of poetics.

Line 119 comes in abruptly:

> aut famam sequere aut sibi convenientia finge.

Read without context, this advice has a more general application than to features of character. Indeed, as we read on, it proves to include plot. But at the moment Horace disguises the shift. He exemplifies his maxim from the field of which he has just been speaking. Just as farmer, nurse and hero had to have appropriate language, because their character is a datum, so the known heroes of mythology must be represented in their accepted colours. A non-traditional character, on the other hand, has merely to obey the law of internal consistency. Now non-traditional *stories* – here is the shift of subject, masked by the common element of breach with tradition – are in fact the clothing of general statements about action and personality in particular forms. *Proprie communia dicere* (128), much disputed, is a more philosophical way of expressing the process more superficially seen by Aristotle as 'adding names'.[17] This is a difficult matter. Better therefore to use traditional stories – but make them your own by distinctive treatment. To illustrate this Horace turns to epic, and gives us an encomium of Homer, in just those respects which most attracted Hellenistic craftsmen – or for that matter Virgil: his sense of how to begin, the plunge *in medias res*, the limitation of the subject, the selection of the poetically viable, the grasp of overall unity. The last point (152) brings us back to the theme of Horace's own exordium. The recollection gives emphasis and a sense of pause, as at the completion of a movement. But the whole passage is, of course, something of a digression. It is a virtuoso piece too: everyone remembers its highlights, the proverbial mouse (139), the alliterative *cum Cyclope Charybdim* (145), the *in medias res* (148).

So back to the stage, to an audience willing to endure to the epilogue (153–5). And back also to the portrayal of character. We seem to be in the situation of ll. 125–8; we are now to hear in more detail how the dramatic *persona* should be maintained. As a teaching example, Horace chooses the Ages of Man. He gives us four:[18] but he bases himself a good deal on the three Ages described from the orator's point of view by Aristotle.[19] Thus Aristotle says of the young:

> They are full of desire and liable to do what they desire.
> Among bodily desires they are most inclined to follow that of sex, in which they have no self-control. They are changeable and fickle in their desires, which they form quickly and give up quickly.

All this comes to half a line:

> cupidusque et amata relinquere pernix (165)

At the same time, there is much in Aristotle for which Horace finds no place: the confidence and hopefulness of the young, their mercifulness, bashfulness, and freedom from disillusion. It is partly of course that these qualities are of interest to the orator, who needs to know how to influence such characters, more than to the poet who has just to represent them; but it is noticeable also that Horace's description has a more satiric tinge, at once vivid and censorious. His timid and grumbling old men, too, show something of this, though the basic features of their character are already in Aristotle. In all this, the poeticizing of the subject involves not only selection but a marked change of tone from the clinical to the satiric.

This connected development is followed, for contrast, by a series of *praecepta* on points of dramatic art. Deliberately not linked, these *praecepta* are varied by the mock-heroic summaries of legends in ll. 185–7, and by the expansive account of the moral attitudes appropriate to a chorus in ll. 196–201.

A taste of such material evidently suffices. If we look ahead, we glimpse a motive for it: the overpowering importance of techniques and observance of the proprieties, which is shortly to be illustrated in a very striking way.

But no signs yet of what is coming. Only a quite natural transition from the chorus to the accompanying music (202). But not the music as it is now: a historical perspective unexpectedly

appears. It is a moralist's view of things, Platonic rather than
Aristotelian, associating prosperity with luxury and, in some
sense, decadence. Aristotle,[20] it is true, had noted that pipe-
playing was introduced into education after the Persian wars; and
also that changes in musical taste were liable to come from the
demands of an uneducated audience. But there is an element in
Horace's account of the theory that moral decline and luxury
were associated: the audience of the later period was no longer
frugi castusque (207). It is reasonable therefore to think of Plato, of
the 'vile theatrocracy' condemned in the *Laws*.[21]

Horace had handled this topic of fifth- and fourth-century
cultural history elsewhere, in the Letter to Augustus.[22] Here he
divorces it from its historical setting. At the same time he touches
it with a master hand: *vino diurno* (209), the matching of oracular
style with sense in ll. 218–19. It is yet another set piece; but not
complete in itself, since it is essential logical preparation for what
follows.

The licentious audience of post-war Greece needed special
titillation at the end of the day;[23] satyr-plays, performed at the
end of sets of tragedies, provided it. This is to choose one of two
rival accounts of the development of drama: not Aristotle's,[24]
according to which tragedy grew as a refined form of the satyr-
play, which is seen as something more primitive; but a later and
commoner one[25] in which Pratinas, a successor of Thespis,
invented satyr-plays as a new variety. Horace's choice – which
may also be Neoptolemus' – is poetically apt, and it is more
important to see this than to wonder about the historical judgment behind it. The story of prosperity and moral laxity leads up
to the new discovery, and the new discovery leads to what is
evidently the end-point of the whole development: namely,
advice on how to write this peculiar genre.

Now there may of course be circumstances which, if known to
us, would reduce our astonishment at this move. The Pisones
may have burned with ambition to conquer even this literary
corner for Rome. Horace may have thought that this was a
desirable step in the progress of Augustan literature. Alexandrian
satyr-plays, such as the *Lityerses* of Sositheos, may have been
notable in themselves or have attracted the attention of the
theorists whom Horace follows. It is in this last point, I am
inclined to say, that the heart of the matter lies. Satyr-drama

aroused special theoretical interest. In its classical form, it was burlesque in content, but tragic in language and metre. This intermediate status called for definition, for a close analysis of metre and style in terms of decorum. It is the consequent rather complicated play with critical concepts that Horace here turns into thirty lines of poetry.

It is a study in balance and the Aristotelian mean. The serious and the humorous must be blended in such a way that heroic characters, already introduced in the serious plays, neither disgrace themselves nor soar above human ken. Satyr-drama is tragedy on holiday, as it were; it is not comedy, for its characters, after all, are divine. It will not eschew metaphor, but it will depend for its distinction on arrangement rather than on unfamiliar language (240–4). This last point is a little strange: it is not true of classical satyr-drama, which has a good deal of exaggerated diction. But Horace is presumably legislating for a refined form of the genre. Finally, the humour must steer clear of the erotic and the indecent. We aim at a respectable audience (248–50).

It would be wrong to suppose that just because this topic occupies a comparatively large space, it is proportionately important in the thematic structure of the poem. We could not after all make a case for this for the Ages of Man. But it would be wrong too to regard the satyr-section as a mere episode. It is too central for that – and not only in position, though it may well be significant that it comes plumb in the middle of the poem. As an illustration of the vital importance of knowledge and technique, it touches the heart of the poem's subject. Moreover, it seems to close a distinct phase in the argument. Little has been said so far to refer us specifically to the Roman situation: ll. 49–58, on vocabulary, seems the only significant exception. With the half-way mark passed, and the satyr-section out of the way, this is to change. Roman problems are dominant in ll. 251–94, prominent also in the rest of the poem.

The organization of ll. 251–94 is not easily missed, and it is important to recognize it. The tongue-in-cheek beginning, as if we did not all know what an iambus was, may mislead for a moment; but it soon becomes obvious that its function is solely to prepare for the point that traditional Roman metrical technique has a crudity and heaviness which are nowadays unforgivable. Modern taste should not accept a Plautine standard of metre – any more than a Plautine standard of humour. Where Rome has done well is in enterprise: not only has she followed Greeks in the successive inventions of tragedy and comedy (275–84), but ventured outside Greek range into historical and Italian plays. Where she fails is in technique: *limae labor et mora*. This alone, apparently, prevents Rome from achieving the traditional praise of the Greeks. Other considerations to come may modify this; but for the moment, the argument seems complete, and the formal address to the Pisones (291–4) both emphasizes the importance of what is said here and signals the end of the main part of the poem.

But even this break, though the most meaningful in the whole composition, is not complete. There is a bridge. Technical perfection in the work has had its emphasis. In what follows, Horace examines the balance of the poet's make-up, and the relation of *ars* to *ingenium* in him. The last part of the poem thus parallels and complements the earlier parts in various ways. None the less it has its independence: it is certainly *de poeta*, and the common comparison with the account of the perfect orator with which Quintilian closes the *Institutio* is an illuminating one. Two features, of very different kinds, give an air of separateness. One is the element of caricature. A welcome butt has presented himself: the poet who relies on his 'genius'. This unpleasing eccentric now keeps cropping up: ll. 295–302, 379–84, 416–18, and especially ll. 453–476. He brings with him a more satirical tone, evident notably in the 'friend and flatterer' development of ll. 422–52. But, second, we have for the first time in the poem an apparent formal division of the material (307–8):

(i) Unde parentur opes, quid alat formetque poetam,
(ii) quid deceat, quid non, (iii) quo virtus, quo ferat error.

The most influential person to take this seriously was Eduard Norden.[26] His identification of (i) with ll. 309–32, (ii) with ll. 333–46, (iii) with l. 347 – end, has been much disputed. But it grows on one; and it, or something like it, must be right.

(i) There is certainly truth in the first part. Here there are three interconnected themes: the practical need of the poet – especially the dramatist – for a knowledge of ethics, and particularly the detailed, preceptive ethics which comes, for example, in treatises *de officiis*; the triumph of a piece that gets character and moral sentiments right over one that is technically competent but trivial;

and the supporting instance of Greece, whose immortal literature is grounded on a moral character free from all greed save greed for fame. This, I think, is the point of the brilliant classroom scene of ll. 325 ff.; Horace is answering an objection which he imagines, but does not spell out: the objection that the emphasis on *mores* in ll. 319–22 seems to conflict with the admiration for Greek technique which is axiomatic in the poem. His answer is that what has been said needs some supplementing: the Greek miracle did not really depend solely on technique, but also on moral qualities, on a generosity and unworldliness not natural to dour, money-grubbing Rome. That meanness is inimical to the growth of literature is a common enough thought: we may compare the last chapter of *De Sublimitate*,[27] where the link between avarice (φιλοχρηματία) and the loss of true standards of excellence is worked out in some detail.

(ii) The reconciliation of the aims of pleasure and utility (333–46) attaches loosely to what precedes: *prodesse* relates to the effect of the *speciosa locis . . . fabula, delectare* to that of the melodious nonsense. But this section has its own coherence. It is a neat, spare little exercise in balances and antitheses: ll. 335–7 take up *prodesse*; ll. 338–40 *delectare*; ll. 341 and 342 repeat the pair; l. 343 states the solution and l. 344 repeats once again: a bland compromise reconciles ψυχαγωγία and διδασκαλία as it does *ingenium* and *ars*.

(iii) But at l. 346 comes a more decided break. We find a string of propositions: (a) small faults are venial; (b) some poetry bears careful and repeated inspection; (c) it's no use being a mediocre poet, though it may be some use being a mediocre lawyer; (d) keep your work eight years before publishing. At first sight, there are contradictions in this, if one takes it all as a recipe for good writing. But it is a whole, and a familiar one. 'Longinus', with different emphasis, combines similar elements: small errors are venial (33–6); great writing sustains repeated study (7); no one would wish to be Apollonius rather than Homer (33).

The appeal to Piso (366), taken up in l. 385, seems to add emphasis to an attitude which, despite the disavowal of obsessive perfectionism, remains somewhat discouraging. Poetry is here a luxury art, and can be compared with the accessories of a good dinner (374–6); we therefore exact a higher standard of perfection than we would in something one might be obliged to do, like speaking in public in a lawsuit. Consequently, if the well-born

Roman attempts it, he should put his efforts aside, submit them to rigorous and friendly critics, and only publish them after long reflection and revision. There may be examples of amateurs who rush in (384–5); these are much to be deprecated.

Piso might surely ask: Why then should I bother to write at all? The answer to this, and the counter as it were to all this discouraging perfectionism, appears in ll. 390–407. The connection here, once again, is a suppressed question, a matter of an imaginary debate, not a textbook sequence of headings. The answer is that the reason for not feeling ashamed of taking endless trouble is that poetry is a very grand thing – a great civilizing force in human history. This is a splendid section: precise, delicate, urbane, steering clear both of the banal and of the pompous. Horace begins with an allegorical version of two myths: Orpheus' taming the savage beasts represents his suppression of cannibalism – or rather, perhaps, of meat-eating; Amphion's miraculous building of Thebes represents (presumably) the power of music to produce order in minds and in society. Lawgiving was thus the first achievement of the ancient *vates*; martial excitement, moral advice, flattery and entertainment followed – in that order.[28]

The ideal poet begins to take shape. A scrupulous but unpedantic craftsman, a balanced moralist and a shrewd observer, he takes his trade seriously because he understands its place in human history. But, by the terms of the poem, he is also a Piso. It is part of the transposition of 'poetics' which the composition of the *Ars* involved that the perfect poet should have the special features of a young Roman nobleman. As the portrait proceeds, this becomes clearer. He must beware of flatterers. Here (419–52) follows a standard topic of ethics, the distinction of flatterer and friend,[29] with a standard Hellenistic illustration.[30] Individuality is given by the reminiscence of Quintilius, the transposition of Aristarchus' obelizing procedures to the critic-friend, and especially by the important *sententia* at the end (451–2):

> hae nugae seria ducent
> in mala . . .

What makes poetry important to a Piso is that his hobby may make him ridiculous. The critic-friend must do his duty.[31]

The final episode of the poem is pure caricature: the enemy is mercilessly traduced; he is not worth keeping alive; goodness knows what impiety has damned him to writing verses; he is a dangerous lunatic – and his recitations spell death.

Set this conclusion side by side with the exordium, and it prompts an observation which may help to bring out the unity of the whole. We began with a monstrous poem; we end with the pseudo-poet who might write it. The *Ars*, with its many facets, the shimmering surface that catches so many different lights, admits of course many observations on this level. But this one is worth more than a moment's pause. It brings out two essentials of the process that turned poetics into this sort of poetry. It reminds us that the *poiēma*, the thing made, could never be material for a poem without the maker, without his emotions and morals, his credibility, his honesty. Only by bringing in the artist could the 'art' be made to live. And second, this particular sort of poem, like the *Satires* and *Epistles*, needs something to laugh about, and, perhaps more important, someone to laugh at. It is the madman who sticks in our mind most, it is the caricature that brings the complicated and allusive artfulness of the whole poem most vividly to life.

The *Ars* is one of those *aurei libelli* treasured in medieval and Renaissance education as containing a particularly potent distillation of the wisdom of antiquity. That it is, in its own right, a subtle, bold and, on the whole, successful poem matters far less historically than its doctrinal content and its apparent utility as a model of a kind of humorous didactic piece. It was for long the most accessible source of the basic tenets of classical criticism: the doctrines of propriety and genre, and the underlying assumption that the poet, like the orator, sets himself a particular task of persuasion and is to be judged by his success in bringing it off. The history of its influence is therefore long and complex; all I can do here, by way of appendix, is to indicate a few points of entry and give a few illustrative extracts from some of the less accessible places.[32]

From the early middle ages, Horace was a curriculum author, and no part of him was more studied than the *Ars*, with its valuable literary lore and its impeccable morality. Medieval poetics, very much an art of the schoolroom, was inevitably much influenced by it: poetical *artes* sprang up which, however different in content, owed their being in the last resort to Horace.[33] In the

Renaissance, imitation took a different road. Girolamo Vida's *Poeticorum Libri III* (1527)[34] is a notable landmark. It was the most famous and successful didactic of the age. Formally, nothing could be much less like the *Ars*. Vida's model is the *Georgics*, his ideal poet is Virgil. There is nothing of Horace's play with theory. Vida's concern is straightforwardly didactic – to teach Virgilian composition, by precept and still more by example. But there are passages of Horatian inspiration, and the basic assumptions of the *Ars* are there. Here, for example, is how Vida handles what is in effect Horace's advice on epic prooemia (II.18–21, 30–9):

> Vestibulum ante ipsum primoque in limine semper
> prudentes leviter rerum fastigia summa
> libant et parcis attingunt omnia dictis
> quae canere statuere: simul caelestia divum
> auxilia implorant, propriis nil viribus ausi . . .
> incipiens odium fugito, facilesque legentum
> nil tumidus demulce animos, nec grandia iam tum
> convenit aut nimium cultum ostentantia fari,
> omnia sed nudis prope erit fas promere verbis:
> ne, si magna sones, cum nondum ad proelia ventum,
> deficias medio irrisus certamine, cum res
> postulat ingentes animos viresque valentes.
> principiis potius semper maiora sequantur:
> protinus illectas succende cupidine mentes
> et studium lectorum animis innecte legendi.

(Before the courtyard, on the very threshold [*Aeneid*, II.469!], the wise always dip lightly into the essentials of the story, and touch on everything they have resolved to sing with a few, sparing words. At the same time, they beg the heavenly help of the gods, for they venture nothing by their own strength. . . . When you begin, avoid causing disgust; have no bombast about you, but soothe your readers' willing ears. At this point it is out of place to talk grandly or in a way that displays too much polish. It will be quite proper to set out everything, almost, in the barest words; if you sound a loud note now, when you have not yet reached the battle, you may well fail ridiculously in the middle of the encounter, when the story demands great courage and powerful strength. Let what follows always be greater than

the beginning. Forthwith inflame the captive mind, with
eagerness, and bind the zeal to read upon your readers' hearts.)

Neologisms are another Horatian theme (III.267–84):

> Nos etiam quaedam idcirco nova condere nulla
> religio vetat indictasque effundere voces.
> ne vero haec penitus fuerint ignota suumque
> agnoscant genus et cognatam ostendere gentem
> possint, ac stirpis nitantur origine certae.
> usque adeo patriae tibi si penuria vocis
> obstabit, fas Graiugenum felicibus oris
> devehere informem massam, quam incude Latina
> informans patrium iubeas dediscere morem.
> sic quondam Ausoniae succrevit copia linguae:
> sic auctum Latium, quo plurima transtulit Argis
> usus et exhaustis Itali potiuntur Athenis.
> nonne vides mediis ut multa erepta Mycenis,
> Graia genus, fulgent nostris immixta, nec ullum
> apparet discrimen? eunt insignibus aequis
> undique per Latios et civis et advena tractus.
> iamdudum nostri cessit sermonis egestas:
> raro uber patriae tibi, raro opulentia deerit.

(No scruple therefore forbids us to invent some new
words, and utter sounds unspoken before. But let them
not be altogether unknown: let them acknowledge their
ancestry, be able to show their relationships, and rely on an
origin in some certain race. If the poverty of our native
vocabulary obstructs you very much, it is right to import
from the happy shores of Greece some shapeless mass which
you can mould on a Latin anvil and command to unlearn its
native ways. This is how the resources of the tongue of
Ausonia grew of old. This is how Latium was developed.
Use transferred many things there from Argos; Italians won
the plunder of an exhausted Athens. Do you not see how
many words, stolen from the heart of Mycenae, Greek in
origin, gleam amid our own? They show no difference; in
like uniform, citizen and stranger move through the realms
of Latium. Our language's poverty has long since yielded;
rarely will the rich soil of your country, rarely its wealth
fail you.)

But the best parts of Vida are perhaps the most independent. The long development on sound and sense towards the end of Book III begins with a reminiscence of Horace, but soon moves away into a sensitive lesson in Virgilian artistry (III.365–76):

> Haud satis est illis utcumque claudere versum,
> et res verborum propria vi reddere claras:
> omnia sed numeris vocum concordibus aptant,
> atque sono quaecumque canunt imitantur, et apta
> verborum facie, et quaesito carminis ore.
> nam diversa opus est veluti dare versibus ora
> diversosque habitus, ne qualis primus et alter,
> talis et inde alter, vultuque incedat eodem.
> hic melior motuque pedum et pernicibus alis
> molle viam tacito lapsu per levia radit:
> ille autem membris ac mole ignavius ingens
> incedit tardo molimine subsidendo.

(It is not enough for them to round off the line anyhow and to make the subject clear by the correct force of the words. They suit everything to harmonious verbal rhythms and imitate the subjects of their song in sounds, with apt shapes of words and a poetical expression diligently sought. For one has as it were to give the lines different expressions and different guises, so that the first is not followed by another and then another of the same kind, moving along with the same look on its face. One is speedier of foot and wing and gently glides over its smooth away with silent motion: another, of mighty limbs and mass, moves more sluggishly, pausing in its slow effort.)

Vida, for all his limitations and pedagogic tone, deserves more attention than he gets. With his concern for practice rather than theory, he follows in a sense in the line of the medieval *artes*; but his Virgilianism and his skill in mimicry are new. Writing in the 1520s, he was still comparatively unaffected by the more profound and speculative poetics that developed from the renewed study of Aristotle.

It was inevitable that, as a source for theory, Horace should take a back seat once the *Poetics* became familiar. He is very much a subsidiary source to the great theorists, a Minturno or a Castelvetro. But he did of course remain popular, and at a somewhat humbler level we see much of his influence in the latter part of the century. G. Fabricius (*De Re Poetica*, 1560) drew up a list of forty-one propositions derived from the *Ars*, with some from the *Epistles* and *Satires*. This proved a popular compendium: William Webbe's *Of English Poetry* (1586) reproduces it.[35] Two of the great literary manifestos of the age also clearly owe a good deal to Horace: du Bellay's *Deffence et Illustration de la langue françoise* (1549) and Sidney's *Apology for Poetry* (1583).[36] But in the field of scholastic poetics, Scaliger's negative judgment was important (*Poetics*, 1561, preface):

> Horatius Artem quam inscripsit adeo sine ulla docet arte
> ut Satyrae propius totum opus illud esse videatur.

And he made himself little use of the *Ars*. Explicitly, or more often tacitly, he criticizes its viewpoints on various matters. His rhetorical prescriptions for the appropriate portrayal of different national characteristics (3.17)[37] and of the Ages of Man (3.15) rest on other sources. For the latter topic, he returns conspicuously to the chapters of Aristotle's *Rhetoric* from which Horace departed.

It is probably broadly true that in the seventeenth century the *Ars* was more important as a poetic model than as a source of critical theory. In England, it attracted Ben Jonson both as commentator (the commentary is lost) and as translator.[38] In France, it served as the model of the most Horatian and most famous of its imitations – Boileau's *Art Poétique* (1674). Boileau's Horatianism is not primarily a matter of the direct allusions, numerous and interesting as these are.[39] It is far more that his insistence on correctness and technique overlaps a good deal, though not completely, with Horace's doctrine of the relation of *ars* and *ingenium*; and that his particular brand of urbanity found the model of the Horatian satire congenial and reasonably well within grasp. There is a difference of tone: more courtliness, less vigour; less conciseness; more obvious order in the layout. But essential Horatian qualities remain, as they do also in Pope's *Essay on Criticism*, where a new slant is given to the traditional material (Vida's as well as Horace's) by concentrating on the function and person of the critic – now not just a friendly and frank Quintilius, but a new sort of professional man.

Horace, we may suspect, would have enjoyed the parodies of himself, or at least some of them, that were a vogue in the eighteenth century. They presuppose the close familiarity with the *Ars* that its use in education so long assured. I quote two excerpts from William King's *Art of Cookery* (1709).[40] First, the Ages of Man (214 ff.):

> If you all sorts of persons would engage,
> Suit well your eatables to ev'ry age.
>   The fav'rite child, that just begins to prattle,
> And throws away his silver bells and rattle,
> Is very humoursome, and makes great clutter
> Till he has windows[41] on his bread and butter;
> He for repeated suppermeat will cry,
> But won't tell mammy what he'd have or why.
>   The smooth fac'd youth that has new guardians chose,
> From playhouse, steps to supper at The Rose,
> Where he a main or two at random throws:
> Squandering of wealth, impatient of advice,
> His eating must be little, costly, nice.
>   Maturer Age, to this delight grown strange,
> Each night frequents his club behind the 'Change,
> Expecting there frugality and health
> And honor, rising from a Sheriff's wealth . . .
>   But then, old age, by still intruding years,
> Torments the feeble heart with anxious fears:
> Morose, perverse in humor, diffident,
> The more he still abounds, the less content;
> His larder and his kitchen too observes,
> And now, lest he should want hereafter, starves;
> Thinks scorn of all the present age can give,
> And none, these threescore years, know how to live.

And this is what King (331 ff.) makes of *Ars*, ll. 270–84:

> Our fathers most admir'd their sauces sweet
> And often ask'd for sugar with their meat;
> They butter'd currants on fat veal bestow'd
> And rumps of beef with virgin-honey strow'd.
> Inspid taste, old Friend, to them who Paris know
> Where rocambole, shalot, and the rank garlic grow.

Tom Bold did first begin the strolling mart
And drove about his turnips in a cart;
Sometimes his wife the citizens would please
And from the same machine sell pecks of pease:
Then pippins did in wheelbarrows abound,
And oranges in whimsey-boards went round.
Bess Hoy first found it troublesome to bawl
And therefore plac'd her cherries on a stall;
Her currants there and gooseberries were spread
With the enticing gold of gingerbread:
But flounders, sprats and cucumbers were cry'd
And ev'ry sound and ev'ry voice was try'd.
At last the law this hideous din supprest,
And order'd that the Sunday should have rest,
And that no nymph her noisy food should sell
Except it were new milk or mackerel.

These *jeux d'esprit* are a proof of the familiarity of the *Ars* to the educated. There is another proof too, perhaps more striking and still with us – the number of phrases of the work that have penetrated our ordinary speech: 'purple patch' (15), *sub iudice* (78), *in medias res* (149), *laudator temporis acti* (173), the mountain giving birth to the mouse (139), Homer nodding (359). All Horace's works have earned this kind of testimony: the *Ars* has it to a rather special degree.

Notes

The literature on the *Ars* is vast. Most recent, and much the most useful guide, is C. O. Brink's *Horace on Poetry* (vol. i, *Prolegomena*, Cambridge, 1963; vol. ii, *Commentary*, 1971). This chapter was written in the main before Brink's *Commentary* was available: I have not made any substantial changes in the light of it. See also G. W. Williams's review of Brink's first volume, *JRS*, 54 (1964), 186–96; and P. Grimal, *Horace: Art Poétique*, Les cours de Sorbonne, 1966. My attempt at a prose translation is in D. A. Russell and M. Winterbottom, *Ancient Literary Criticism*, Oxford, 1971, pp. 279–91.

1 Praef, 2, 8.3.60.
2 Cf. Demetrius, 228: συγγράμματα τὸ χαίρειν ἔχοντα προσγεγραμμένον.
3 For recent discussion see R. Syme, *JRS*, 1960, 12–20.
4 Tacitus, *Ann.*, VI.10.
5 Varro indeed is better placed to help us, for he tells us facts of ancient rural life which we need to know. The theorist Neoptolemus unlocks no such stores of otherwise unattainable knowledge.

6 *Rep.*, 392.

7 See esp. Brink, op. cit., pp. 59 ff.

8 Ibid., p. 58.

9 Cf. 'Longinus' 2.

10 H. Peacham, *The Compleat Gentleman* (1622).

11 Plutarch, *Moralia*, 346 F.

12 See, e.g. 'Longinus' 3, Demetrius, 114, [Cicero] *ad Herennium* IV, for 'adjacent faults' of various kinds.

13 Or to 44, if Bentley's transposition of *hoc amet, hoc spernat* . . . to follow *in verbis* . . . *serendis* is right, as (e.g.) Vahlen, Kiessling-Heinze, and Brink maintain.

14 Donatus, *vita*, 44: 'novae cacozeliae repertorem, non tumidae nec exilis [i.e. not arising from the common perversions of the grand and simple styles] sed ex communibus verbis atque ideo latentis.'

15 Cf. Aristotle, *Rhetoric*, 3.7.

16 *Moralia*, 853D. The parallel confirms the reading *divus* in 114.

17 *Poetics*, 1451b10.

18 Cf. in general F. Boll, *Die Lebensalter, Neue Jahrbücher* XXXI, 89–146 (1913), reprinted in *Kleine Schriften zur Sternkunde des Altertums*, Leipzig, 1950.

19 *Rhetoric*, 2.12–14.

20 *Politics*, 1341^a 28, ^{b}15.

21 700 A–701 B. But see Cicero, *De Legibus*, 2.38.

22 *Epist.*, 11.1. 93 ff.

23 Cf. ll. 154–5 for the idea of 'keeping' the audience till the end of the performance.

24 *Poetics*, 1449^a 20, if this is the right interpretation of ἐκ σατυρικοῦ μεταβαλεῖν. Cf. also Dioscorides, *Anth. Pal.*, VII.37.1–6.

25 *Suda*, s.v. 'Pratinas'.

26 *Hermes*, 40 (1905), 481–525.

27 'Longinus' 44.6–7.

28 A verbal – but hardly significant – contradiction of l. 377: *animis natum* . . . *poema iuuandis.*

29 See especially Plutarch's *De adulatore et amico.*

30 Diodorus, 20.63.1

31 Not to do so would be to yield to a pernicious inhibition, what Greek moralists called δυσωπία: cf. *pudens prave* (l. 88.)

32 See, besides the standard general histories of criticism: J. E. Spingarn, *A History of Literary Criticism in the Renaissance*, New York, 1908; B. Weinberg, *History of Literary Criticism in the Italian Renaissance*, Chicago, 1961; M. T. Herrick, *The Fusion of Horatian and Aristotelian Literary Criticism, 1531–1555*, New York, 1946.

33 On Matthew of Vendôme's *Ars versificatoria* and Geoffrey of Vinsauf's *Poetria nova*, see F. J. E. Raby, *Secular Latin Poetry*, ii, 30, 122; E. Faral, *Les arts poétique du XIIe and XIIIe siècle*, Paris, 1923; J. de Ghellinck, *L'essor de la littérature latine au XIIe siècle*, Brussels, 1946, ii, 243 ff.

34 Many editions down to the eighteenth century. An excellent English verse translation was made by Christopher Pitt (1725).

35 Text in G. Gregory Smith, *Elizabethan Critical Essays*, vol. i (1904), Oxford, 290 ff. (English), 417 ff. (Latin).

36 The standard editions give the necessary information: Sidney is in Gregory Smith, op. cit., i, 148 ff., for du Bellay see the edn of H. Chamard, Paris, 1945. In du Bellay, note especially: 2.4. Ly donques et rely premierement . . . feuillete de main nocturne et journelle les exemplaires grecs et latins: 2.4 te fourniront de matière les louanges des Dieux et des hommes vertueux, le discours fatal des choses mondaines, la solicitude des jeunes hommes, comme l'amour: les vins libres, et toute bonne chere: 2.6 ne crains donques . . . d'innover quelques termes . . . avecques modestie toutefois . . . Du Bellay's Latinisms were severely attacked in a pamphlet published in 1550, 'le Quintil Horatian', which takes its title from Horace's critic-friend.

37 Cf. *AP*, l. 118. Only *Assyrii* occur of Horace's examples. It is tempting to cite some of the rest:
Germani fortes, simplices, animarum prodigi, veri amici, verique hostes. Suetii, Noruegii, Gruntlandii, Gotti, beluae. Scoti non minus. Angli perfidi, inflati, feri, contemptores, stolidi, amentes, inertes, inhospitales, immanes . . .

38 *Works*, ed Herford and Simpson, viii, 303 ff.

39 E.g. 1.11 (*AP*, 38); 1.64 (*AP*, 31); 1.77 (*AP*, 343); 1.190 (*AP*, 424); 3.61 ff. (origin of tragedy); 3.124 (*AP*, 125); 3.269 ff. (*AP*, 136 ff.); 3.375 ff. (ages of man – omits childhood); 4.26 (*AP* 372); 4.71 ff. (the good critic); 4.135 ff. (civilizing effect of poetry).

40 For the author's character, see Johnson's *Life*.

41 I.e. patterns made with sugar on the bread.

VI

'The Best of Lyrick Poets'

Valerie Edden

Horace, the Best of Lyrick Poets ran the title of a volume of translations of selected odes and epodes of Horace which was published in 1652, echoing *The Lyrick Poet* of John Smith three years earlier. The title seems in no way remarkable to those of us who have learned to love Horace's lyric poetry even in our schooldays. But it is a significant title for it marks a change in attitude to Horace, for from the beginning of the Christian era until the early seventeenth century Horace was read (when he was read at all) as a moralist, not as a lyric poet. This essay surveys the vicissitudes of Horace's reputation in England, from the early period in which he was regarded primarily as a satirist until his final acceptance as a lyric poet in the seventeenth century, and discusses the English translations produced before 1670.

It was to be expected that Horace would not rank high among the Roman authors most loved in the early Christian era. The classics had for centuries an ambiguous position in the Christian culture of the Latin West; at worst they merited complete condemnation, at best they were tolerated for the sake of their morality (where it could be put to the service of Christianity) and to provide examples of rhetorical usages:[1]

Quid facit cum psalterio Horatius? cum evangeliis Maro? cum apostolo Cicero?

(What has Horace to do with the Psalter, or Virgil with the gospels or Cicero with the Apostle?)

asks Jerome accusingly, though he (like so many others then and later) loved the pagan writers he so fiercely condemned, and produced elaborate justifications for reading them. But Horace was always third behind Virgil and Ovid and often a very poor third. Horace's peculiar excellence consists of qualities which were not much admired in late antiquity and the middle ages; the concision and delicacy, his capacity to be 'plenus . . . iucunditatis et gratiae et varius figuris et verbis felicissime audax' (full of delight and charm, with great variety in his use of figures, bold in his choice of words, but happily so) which Quintilian commended,[2] were increasingly difficult to appreciate as the Latin of the Augustan era became more and more remote from the version of that language actually in use. Similarly the subtlety and variety of metre used by Horace in his *Odes* earned little admiration from men who barely understood the rules of classical prosody, as their imitations of classical models prove; Bede's *De Arte Metrica*, which is a fairly typical treatise, misunderstands the nature of quantitative stress almost entirely. The wit, humour and urbanity may have privately delighted the classical scholar competent to appreciate them, but were not likely to receive much attention from schoolmasters. And it was through use in the schools that Latin poetry survived.

Perhaps Virgil and Ovid suffered from similar disadvantages to a certain extent, but these two poets were capable of adaptation for Christian use in ways which were not possible with Horace. Virgil's fourth *Eclogue* was commonly interpreted as an unwitting prophecy of the birth of Christ, so Virgil was hailed as a saintly figure whose virtue made him worthy to receive such a revelation. Men who habitually allegorized the Scriptures were easily able to allegorize the *Aeneid* and the *Metamorphoses*, but only works with a strong narrative line are susceptible to allegorization and there are no attempts to allegorize any of Horace's poems, as far as I know, and it is difficult to envisage how such a task might have been achieved.

Where Horace was read at all, it was not the *Odes* but the *Satires* and *Epistles* which were known, and of the satirists, Juvenal was frequently preferred to Horace, presumably because he is sharper, more direct and cutting. The two authors most commonly linked with Horace are Juvenal and Persius, whose poems are often contained in the same volume, a tradition which continued even as late as the seventeenth century.

It is difficult to assess how widely any author was known in late antiquity and the middle ages. Quotations and allusions may be at second-hand only. Extant manuscripts are few and far between and can represent but a tiny proportion of the manuscripts which once existed. Contemporary library catalogues are often known to be incomplete, and even when apparently full often cite only an author's name rather than the works by which he is represented. So it is with this caveat in mind that I summarize briefly the availability of Horace in England in this early period.

We can deduce something of the extent to which Horace was known in Anglo-Saxon England from the fact that allusions to all his works have been found in the writings of Anglo-Saxon authors.[3] However it is difficult to know whether these allusions derive from first-hand knowledge or came through patristic writers (many men certainly derived much of their classical learning from Jerome), or from florilegia, anthologies of passages from poems which usually contained both Christian and classical authors, and in which Horace was represented by maxims drawn from the *Satires* and *Epistles*. Bede (673–735) alludes to Horace occasionally in his youthful writings, but Virgil alone of classical authors figures in later works.[4] Whether or not Alcuin (735–804) knew him at first-hand has been a matter of dispute, though it was as 'Flaccus' that Horace was known when the learned men who were in the circle of Charlemagne (including Theodulf of Orleans, Modoin and Paulinus of Aquileia) all adopted literary nicknames. But Horace is not included in those authors listed by Alcuin as being in the library at York;[5] the omission is surprising since not only Virgil is mentioned but Lucan and Statius also. However Alcuin certainly knew the *Ars Poetica*, since the commentary on that work known as the *Scholia Vindobonensia* is sometimes ascribed to Alcuin himself, and was certainly produced in his circle.[6]

Possibly Alcuin gained his knowledge of the Roman poet on the Continent, where Horace was certainly known at first-hand in the mid-ninth century if not in Alcuin's lifetime. The famous Bern Horace (*Bern 363*) dates from the late ninth century and Horace is included in several catalogues of Continental libraries of the Carolingian era; Manitius gives four instances of Horace's manuscripts dating from this period.[7] There was a manuscript of Horace at Lorsch,[8] and at Fleury in the tenth century (though a catalogue from Fleury a century earlier mentions only Virgil and Terence among pagan authors),[9] though surprisingly, not at Bobbio.[10]

Horace gained a new popularity in the eleventh and twelfth centuries, with the revival of classical studies and the vogue for satire, as a consequence of which the *Odes* still took second place to the *Satires* and *Epistles*. In comparison with the four ninth-century manuscripts already mentioned, Manitius finds thirty-four in the eleventh century and thirty-seven in the twelfth.[11] Other Roman satirists (notably Juvenal and Persius) had a similar rise in popularity.

Of the libraries of this period M. D. Knowles writes:[12]

> Horace is very frequent, though the Odes less so than the Satires and Epistles. Manitius finds him in nine houses (Canterbury had ten copies in 1170 and Dover five, with commentaries in addition, in 1389). Mynors adds six more copies.

It was at this time that Horace became once more a standard curriculum-author, a position he had held in antiquity and which he maintained until recent times. Gerbert (later to become Pope Sylvester II) had lectured on him in the schools in the tenth century, but he cannot be said to be firmly established in England or on the Continent until the twelfth century. He is included in a school-curriculum drawn up by Alexander Neckham[13] (1157–1217), who settled as a schoolmaster in Dunstable after lecturing in Paris. Neckham is unusual in commending all of Horace's works, otherwise his list of authors is similar to that in use on the Continent. Conrad of Hirsau (*c.* 1070–1150) includes Horace along with Virgil, Sallust and Cicero as the only classical authors in a list of twenty-one authors, but recommends only the *Ars Poetica* unconditionally, and in the next century Eberhard the German (fl. before 1180) recommends the *Satires* only.[14]

The comparative popularity of the separate works is indicated by Hugo of Trimberg (*c.* 1230–*c.*1313):[15]

> Sequitur Horatius, prudens et discretus,
> Vitiorum emulus, firmus et mansuetus;
> Qui tres libros etiam fecit principales,
> Duosque dictaverat minus usuales;
> Epodon videlicit, et librum odarum,
> Duos nostris temporibus credo valere parum.

(Then follows Horace, wise and discerning, enemy of vices, unyielding yet mild, who wrote three main books; and he wrote also two less common works, called the *Epodes* and the book of *Odes*; I believe these two are not popular in our days).

He is included in the list of books known to Boston of Bury;[16] and that great English scholar of the twelfth century, John of Salisbury (*c.* 1115–80), makes frequent use of Horace, particularly for his moral maxims, and includes him with Juvenal and Persius under the heading of 'poetae ethici'.

Throughout the later middle ages Horace was read as a school-text, admired for the morality of the *Satires*. His popularity grew as education became more readily available with the foundation of the grammar schools in the Renaissance. Erasmus included Horace (along with Virgil, Cicero, Caesar, Terence and Sallust) in his list of books suitable for school use in *De Ratione Studii*, and this list apparently influenced his friend Colet, when approving the curriculum for use at St Paul's. Unlike Virgil, whose *Eclogues* were taught at elementary level and whose *Aeneid* provides the material for advanced study, the study of Horace was normally confined to the universities and the higher classes of the grammar schools.[17] We can learn something of the comparative popularity of Horace among students and scholars in Oxford in 1520 from the list of sales in John Dorne's *Day Book*, which cites thirty-seven copies of Cicero and Terence, thirty of Aristotle, twenty-nine of Virgil, twenty-three of Ovid, fourteen of Lucan and only eight of Horace.[18]

The *Odes* as well as the *Satires* were read in the schools, though they were perhaps widely known from fragments quoted in grammar books, as is well known from *Titus Andronicus*:[19]

Demetrius	What's here? a scroll; and written round about;
	Let's see:
	Integer vitae, scelerisque purus,
	Non eget Mauri iaculis, nec arcu.
Chiron	O, 'tis a verse in Horace; I know it well:
	I read it in the grammar long ago.

The grammar book referred to is probably Lily's Latin Grammar, in which these lines from *Carm.*, I.22 occur twice, though only once ascribed to Horace. But if it is true, as has been claimed, that Shakespeare's knowledge of Horace conforms to that supposed ordinarily to be acquired in grammar school, then it is interesting that not a single allusion to the *Satires* has been found in his plays, whilst allusions to the *Odes* are comparatively frequent, although there was at that time no English translation of the *Odes*. [20]

The revival of interest in the *Odes* in England had long been anticipated in France and Italy. Petrarch had hailed Horace

> Salve o dei lirici modi sovrano,
> Salve o degl'Italia gloria ed onor

(Hail, O sovereign of the lyric measure, hail Italy's glory and honour), and Mancinelli's edition of the *Odes*, *Epodes* and *Carmen Saeculare* in 1492 was received with acclaim and reprinted many times. The first full translation of the *Odes* into French, that of Mondot in 1579, predated the first English translation by nearly fifty years.

The distinction of being the first English translator of Horace fell to Lewis Evans, who translated the *Satires* in 1565. Unfortunately Evans's translations are not now available. His extant writings are all in the field of religious controversy, and it may well be that his interest in Horace sprang from a desire to use his satirical writings to censure the vices of his own time.

This was certainly true of another early translator, Thomas Drant (d. 1578). Drant, who was Archdeacon of Lewes, wrote many verses in Greek and Latin, and may have translated other classical authors, though translations of Horace are the only ones to survive. [21] In 1566 he published *A Medicinable Morall*, in which translations of the *Satires* joined with the Lamentations of Jeremiah to point the folly of submitting to passion, a lesson which was driven home forcefully in the Preface. Drant explained his choice of authors by saying that Jeremiah weeps at sin whilst Horace laughs at it. These verses are not so much translations as paraphrases, 'Englyshed according to the prescription of Saint Hierome

> Quod malum est, muta
> Quod bonum est, prode.

(Change that which is evil, publish that which is good)

(Jerome is of course echoing Romans 12:9).

It would seem that *A Medicinable Morall* whetted Drant's appetite for Horace, and 1567 saw the publication of a translation of the *Satires, Epistles* and the *Art of Poetry*. He had been reading Lambinus' commentary, which had been published in Leiden in 1561, and now found Horace admirable, not for his moral worth alone, but also as a poet, and in his Preface praised him for having himself that blend of *utile* and *dulce* which he commended in the *Ars Poetica*, 'If we wey both profytte and delectation Lambinus wrote truly, amongst Latin poets Horace hath not his felowe.' But we can deduce from Drant's comments that he felt uneasy at being associated with a poet whose love-poems at least were of little worth in the perennial battle against evil, and he writes as if on the defensive 'Neither be the things in him lighte trifles . . . he hath good, sounde, deepe, massye [weighty] and wel rellest [transferred?] stuffe.'

This time he aimed at a precise and accurate translation: 'I have translated him sumtymes at Randum. And nowe at this time welnye worde for word.' But he was obliged to acknowledge himself not really equal to the task, explaining at length in the Preface what difficulties beset him. 'There is none of my time, and progresse in scholes would have taken this author in hande, because the paines is great, and the gaynes not greate.' One undoubted source of difficulty which Drant does not mention is his use of the cumbersome fourteener; it is difficult to imagine any metre less suitable for conveying the Roman poet's graceful and subtle rhythms, though by confining himself to the *Satires* and *Epistles*, Drant does not have to attempt to convey the metrical variety of the *Odes*. Drant faces that eternal problem of translators of Horace: translating from an inflected language into an uninflected one always poses problems, for nuances that are conveyed by word order in the one have to be spelt out in full in the other; with a writer as concise as Horace, the problem is even greater. Either the English version is twice as long as the original or else the Latin loses much of its richness and subtlety in translation. Drant, with his long line, sacrifices brevity to fulness: his desire to translate to the letter leads him into clumsiness and unnatural syntax, as the opening lines of *Epist.*, II.1. 1–20 show:

> Since thou sustaines such bussness
> and so much bringste abowte

Defends the Itale realme wyth armes,
 with mannors[22] sets it out,
Reformes with lawes: I shold but do
 the common wealth much wrong
If I shoulde stay thy well-spente time,
 Cesar, with talking long.
Both Romulus, and God Bacchus,
 Pollux, and Caster to
For valiante feates of chiualrie
 Saintes shryned long ago,
Whilst they made their abode on earthe
 Emongste us mortal men,
Stayde warres, built townes, and laide out fieldes,
 they much compleined then,
That honor such so plawsible
 did not ensew their acts,
As they did thinke they had deserued
 by merits and their factes.

Drant errs here on the side of expansion rather than omission
(though he does omit *solus* and *aspera*); the last five half-lines
cover one and a half lines of Latin adding only very little to the
sense: there seems nothing in the original to account for 'such so
plawsible', and 'and their facts' seems to have been added for the
sake of the rhyme. In spite of all Drant's protestations of literal-
ness, he transforms 'post ingentia facta deorum in templa recepti';
the mythological characters become typical heroes of Romance,
who combine valour and piety.

 Sixty years passed between Drant's translation and the next
major translation of Horace. *Certain Selected Odes of Horace
Englisht by John Ashmore* appeared in 1621. Of John Ashmore we
know little; no other work of his remains. He was probably a
Yorkshireman.[23] Like Drant, who had been inspired by Lambinus' commentary, Ashmore's admiration for Horace stemmed
from reading the comments of Julius Caesar Scaliger, whose
notes are recorded sporadically.

 The *Odes* selected by Ashmore show clearly the change of taste
since the 1560s; the prefatory verses announce 'These lyrick
Poet's songs . . . Tun'd (as I could) to my Pipe's homely laies.'
Of the odes chosen, four are love-songs and five are concerned

with poetry itself; to these are added two in praise of the simple
life, two chosen for the nobility of their sentiment (*Carm.*, II.10
on the virtue of moderation, and *Carm.*, 1.22, whose opening
stanza, with its apparently high moral tone, probably misled
unwary readers then as it does now[24]), the Postumus Ode
(II.14), which, with its profound sadness at the transience of
human life, touches on a theme always dear to the Anglo-Saxon
heart, and *Carm.*, IV.7, which treats of the same theme though with
a different emphasis. The collection is neatly balanced and opens
and closes (as did Horace's own collection of odes when it was
first published in three books only) with 1.1 and III.30. In addition
to these odes, Ashmore includes *Epode* II, which he entitles
Laudes rei rusticae. He adds an Appendix of translations of other
poems praising the simple life.[25]

Ashmore's translations have not been well received in modern
times; 'Ashmore's poetry is admittedly poor', writes Miss
Røstvig,[26] and compares him unfavourably with Cowley, whose
translations 'are as inspired as those of Ashmore's are humdrum'.[27] But he deserves credit for more than merely being
the first English translator of the *Odes*. Writing throughout in
regular iambic pentameters and usually in rhymed couplets, his
verses are open to the charge of monotony, but as translations
they are not entirely unsuccessful; the unpretentiousness which
Miss Røstvig finds humdrum rises at best to a simplicity which
contrasts sharply with some of the over-sophisticated versions
later in the century. Though he does not claim to translate
literally, he is in fact more careful and accurate than Drant, and
is often sensitive to Horace's precise meaning. He is remarkable
among early translators for keeping the emphatic repetitions of the name Postumus at the beginning of *Carm.*, II.14,
and his 'sad cyparess' (*invisas cupressos*) is lifted by many late
translators of this line. (The epithet is of course commonplace in English,[28] but particularly apt in this line of Horace for all
that.) Where he cannot convey the exact shade of meaning in one
word, he usually employs a phrase to avoid losing the implications of the original; thus *labuntur* (*Carm.*, II.14.2), because of
its association with the movement of a river, becomes 'doe passe
away like glyding streames', and in the same ode, *linquenda* (21)
becomes 'thou needs must leave.' 'High-spirited wine' is an
attempt to keep the hypallage of *superbo mero* (*Carm.*, II.14.25–6),

but is hardly successful. On occasion he substitutes for Horace's word a contemporary equivalent; we cannot tell how much these words jarred at the time, but they certainly seem bizarre to the twentieth-century ear; perhaps the worst of these modernizations is 'cod-piec't breeches' for *vestimenta* (*Carm.*, 1.5.16).

The following ode is typical of Ashmore's achievement and deficiencies and compares very favourably with Fanshawe's version (discussed below) (*Carm.*, 1.13. 1–20):

> When Lydia thou of Telephus dost tell
> His rosie neck and plyant armes dost praise,
> My liver then (alas!) begins to swell,
> Enrag'd with wrath which nothing can appease.
>
> My colour, changing oft, doth plainely shew
> How my perplexed minde is plung'd in woe:
> And tears by stealth from watry eyes that flowe,
> Can nothing quench loves fire that still doth growe.
>
> I vexed am, whether [w]arre-breeding wine
> Caus'd roaring Boyes to wrong thy shoulders faire;
> Or the Lust-raging Lad, those lips of thine
> The wanton marke caus'd of his tooth to beare.
>
> Beleeve me, he will never constant prove,
> That rudely wrongs sweet kisses in such sort;
> Those kisses which the Goddess faire of loue
> Graceth with the fift part of her best sport.
>
> Thrice happy, and more happy, are they sure,
> Whose mutuall love so banisheth all strife,
> That pure and constant it doth still endure
> Till Fates cut off their well-spun thread of life.

This is at times more paraphrase than translation, though only once does Ashmore attempt to embellish his original, when his lover's tears quench the fire of love, a conceit which might have appealed in the 1620s, but which is scarcely Horatian. The poem presents difficulties which the translator does not always meet: in England we have never much valued a young man's *cervicem roseam*, and 'his rosie neck' though accurate enough, hardly enhances the description; the *cerea bracchia* surely referred to smooth skin rather than pliant or supple limbs, (but how preferable to Fanshawe's 'Arms that wax-like bend'). But he keeps the emphasis of *felices ter et amplius*, (compare Fanshawe's weak 'O their felicitee'), and whilst altering the syntax and the figure, the final stanza is near to Horace in spirit. No doubt many people still believed that the liver was the seat of the passions and could accept without demur the *fervens iecur* which proves so difficult to the modern translator. Ashmore misses the link between the final *ignibus* of the second stanza, and the opening *Uror* ('I burn') of the third.

Ashmore's translation was soon followed by that of Sir Thomas Hawkins (d. 1640), a staunch Catholic and recusant. The first edition in 1627 contained twenty-six odes and five epodes; it proved very popular and was followed by three further editions in 1631, 1635 and 1638, each correcting and expanding the previous one; the 1638 volume contained sixty-four odes and eight epodes.

On the whole Hawkins's translations are not superior to those of Ashmore. They suffer from the same monotonous regularity of metre, though iambic pentameter is varied with iambic tetrameter, and this dull regularity draws attention to itself when time and time again the natural sentence-order is disrupted for the sake of the rhyme or the metre (*Carm.*, 1.15.5–10).

> Thou her tak'st home with thee in an ill hower,
> Whom Greece shall fetch again with armed power,
> Conspiring to dissolve thy married state,
> And Priam's antient Kingdome ruinate.
> Alas! what toil for horse, for men what pain,
> What direful funerals of Trojans slain.

He is quite literal, translating single epithets by single words, and often even reproducing the syntax of the original (*Carm.*, 1.31. 3–15)

> Not the rich corn of fat Sardinia,
> Nor gratefull flocks of burnt Calabria,
> Nor gold, nor Indian ivorie; nor the grounds,
> Which silent Lyris with soft stream arrounds. [29]
> Let those to whom Fortune so much store assigns,
> Prime with Calenian hook their fertile vines:
> Let the rich merchant to the Gods so dear,
> (For so I term him right, who every year,
> Three, or four times, visits the Atlantique seas.)

Here every word is translated and the only embellishment is 'fertile' (for the sake of the metre); the repeated 'not, nor' reproduces exactly the repeated *non* of the original, and Hawkins adds a further one still, translating *aut* also as 'nor'. *Opima Sardinia* becomes, unhappily, 'fat Sardinia', for although 'fat' is appropriate for *opimus* when applied to cattle, when applied to land it clearly calls for 'fruitful' or 'fertile'; the choice of 'fat' seems again to be determined by the metre. Similarly, and most unfortunately, is 'burnt' Calabria for *aestuosus*, 'sultry' though the metre would not have precluded 'hot'. This translation as a whole is uninspired and uninspiring.

Carm., 1.11 is somewhat more successful; Hawkins's pentameters are more appropriate for the long lines of the fifth asclepiad than they are for Horace's other metres.

> Strive not (Leuconoe) to know what end
> The Gods above to thee or me will send:
> Nor with Astrologers consult at all,
> That thou may'st better know what can befall.
> Whether, thou liv'st more winters, or thy last
> Be this, which Tyrren waves 'gainst rocks do cast
> Be wise, drink free, and in so short a space,
> Do not protracted hopes of life embrace.
> Whilest we are talking, envious Time doth slide:
> This day's thine own, the next may be deny'd.

But over all it is timorous and unimaginative, making no attempt at *scire nefas* nor at *oppositis*, missing the tense of *fugerit* ('will have passed') and perhaps weakest of all 'This day's thine own' for Horace's *Carpe diem*.

1638, the year which produced the fourth version of Hawkins's translation, also produced the first complete translation of the *Odes*, by Henry Rider (b. 1606). In strong contrast to Hawkins, Rider was a Protestant with Puritan leanings, a graduate of Emmanuel College, Cambridge. The volume is dedicated to the Puritan Lord Rich, Second Earl of Warwick. As was to be expected, Rider felt a little uneasy at the lack of high moral seriousness in some of Horace's *Odes*, but the fact that he did not translate the *Satires* and *Epistles* reveals that his real interest lay not so much in the matter of the poems, but in Horace's poetic skill. 'You will find many Odes which have little or no matter in them, as being composed by the prime author onely to shew the excellence of the Roman phrase, and verse; others mixt of words and matter; many materially excellent'. And he refers to Horace as one who 'either learned from, or taught the Spheres a perfect musicall harmonie, and made the language of Rome truly Roman'.

Rider is scholarly in his approach to translation; in the Preface, he discusses the difficulties which he had encountered and how he had attempted to solve them. These are all difficulties of interpretation in which the commentators had disagreed on Horace's precise meaning. He writes also of the problem of translating into a single English word a Latin word which carries undertones as well as its obvious meaning. Unfortunately the example he chooses is of a word not now thought to be ambiguous (*Carm.*, 1.35. 11–12):

> Regumque matres barbarorum et
> purpurei metuunt tyranni.

Where the word *purpurei* may be understood of the cruelty of tyrants, whose hands are dipt in blood; or the royale clothings of Kings and Emperours in purple robes: in the former sense I have translated the words thus

> And barbarous Kings mothers are afeard
> And tyrants too with purple gore besmear'd.

In the latter sense it may be thus rendered,

> And barbarous kings mothers are afraid,
> And tyrants too with purple robes araid.[30]

His translations share the faults of his predecessors'. Difficulties attended his attempts to fit Horace's meaning into rhymed couplets; like Ashmore and Hawkins before him, he uses mainly iambic pentameters, though he varies these with tetrameters. At their worst, his translations, like theirs, are unidiomatic, with an unnatural sentence-order (III.17. 1–4, 13–16):

> O Aelius from ancient Lamus fam'd
> (Whence the first Lamia, they say, were nam'd,
> And every house of your posteritie,
> Through all records yet kept in memorie).
>   . . .

> While you may, your drie wood together put;
> Your corps tomorrow you with wine must glut,
> And with a porcling just of two months old,
> With all thy men from labour bid to hold.'

His Pyrrha ode (*Carm.*, 5)[31] suffers from being somewhat too literal (9–16):

> Who hopes thou'lt still be free to him, still faire,
> Ignorant of thy all-deluding aire.
> Wretched are they to whom untride you shine;
> The wall, by sacred tables made divine,
> Shewes I have hung my ship-rackt robe on high
> Unto the Oceans potent Deitie.

His 'ship-rackt robe' avoids the issue of the difficult *uvida vestimenta*. Elsewhere in the ode, he translates *simplex munditiis* as 'plain in your ornament', which hardly conveys what Horace intended, but his 'tender boy' (for *gracilis puer*) is certainly superior to Dr Holyday's 'spritely younker'.

   With Ben Jonson we come to the first translation of Horace by a major British poet. His translation of the *Ars Poetica* was first published posthumously in 1640, in an early draft in John Benson's duodecimo collection of the poems and then in a revised draft in the second volume of the folio. Jonson was a great admirer of Horace throughout his life, and unlike most of his contemporaries, found something of interest and benefit in each of his works. The playwright who aimed in his own plays to correct the follies and vices of his own time by ridicule found Horace's satire and social criticism congenial; the Roman writers which Jonson commended to Drummond of Hawthornden included Horace, Tacitus, Juvenal and Martial, and it was as a satirist that Horace appears in *The Poetaster* (1601). As a lyric poet who had tried his own hand at odes, Jonson particularly valued Horace's lyric poems, and in his 'Ode to Himself' (1629), written on the censure of *The New Inne*, he writes affectionately of Horace:

> Leaue things so prostitute,
> And take the Alcaick Lute;
> Or thine owne Horace, or Anacreon's Lyre
> Warme thee, by Pindares fire.

Indeed one can but agree with his editors:[32]

In his Horatian conciseness and sobriety, and in his Horatian power of pregnant and impressive ethical statement, lay indeed his principal asset as a maker of odes; and such virtue as his own possess is chiefly of this kind. He himself knew where his affinity lay, if he hardly recognised his limitations. He might borrow the Alcaic lute, and 'warm himself by Pindar's fire', but Horace was his own.

The *Ars Poetica* had enjoyed wide popularity ever since the sixteenth century, and it was widely known and read in the original. Jonson writes of his admiration for Horace in *Discoveries*, when discussing the 'office of a true critic or Censor': 'Such was Horace, an Author of much Civilitie; and (if any one among the heathen can be) the best master, both of vertue, and wisdome; an excellent, and a true judge upon cause, and reason; not because he thought so; but because he knew so, out of use and experience.'[33] His translation is remarkable for a concise, epigrammatic quality:[34]

> The Muse not only gave the Greek's a wit,
> But a well-compass'd mouth to utter it.

and:

> Let what thou fain'st for pleasure's sake, be neere
> The Truth, nor let thy Fable think what e're
> It would, must be: lest it alive would draw
> The Child, when Lamia has dined out of her maw.

But where Jonson really excels is in his other translations of Horace, that is of *Odes*, III.9 and IV.1 and the second Epode. Whilst adhering faithfully to the Latin, his translations are fluent and idiomatic, indeed his translation of the second Epode undoubtedly ranks as a fine poem in its own right (9–20):

> The Poplar tall, he then doth marrying twine
> With the growne issue of the Vine;
> And with his hooke lops off the fruitlesse race,
> And sets more happy in the place:
> Or in the bending[35] Vale beholds a-farre
> The lowing herds there grazing are:
> Or the prest honey in pure pots doth keepe
> Of earth, and sheares the tender Sheepe;

Or when that Autumne, through the Fields, lifts round
His head, with mellow Apples crown'd,
How plucking Peares, his own hand grafted had,
And purple-matching Grapes, hee's glad. [36]

During the next few decades there were new translations of
Horace's works. In 1649 John Smith published his translation
of the *Odes* and *Satires*, but his translation did not supersede
Hawkins's, which was reissued partially three years later, together
with a translation of Persius Flaccus by Barton Holyday, under
the title *Horace the best of Lyrick Poets*.

Holyday, a graduate of Oxford, his native city, translated
Juvenal as well as Persius Flaccus and in 1653 produced an
anonymous translation of the *Odes, All Horace His Lyrics*. This
volume has acquired an undeserved notoriety, since from an
early date there has been a belief that Holyday was merely
reprinting Hawkins's translations. [37] In 1666 Alexander Brome
wrote in his collection of translations of Horace: 'What were
omitted by [Fanshawe], I supplied with such as have been done
by Sir Thomas Hawkins or Dr. Holyday, or both, for they are
both the same and whether of the two is the author, remains to
me undiscovered.' The two translations are in fact quite different.

Holyday's main concern was with Horace's metre. Although
all previous translators had confined themselves to conveying
Horace's meaning in common English metres, those who studied
Horace in the original (from schoolboys to eminent scholars)
paid particular attention to his metre and early printed editions
of Horace usually contained prefatory material explaining the
different metres used. It was almost inevitable that Holyday
should flounder in attempting to reproduce classical metres in
English; many men have tried since and no one has yet achieved
any real measure of success. Holyday's attempts are interesting
for their curiosity value; in *Carm.*, 1.36 he attempts to recreate
the second asclepiad (1–6):

> With Frankincense and Lyric Lay,
> And bullocks justly slaughter'd, let's allay
> Great Numia's tutelary Gods:
> Who safe arriv'd from Spain's remot'st abodes,
> Gave's dear friends many a – kiss – salute,
> But to sweet Lamia most did distribute.

Unfortunately Holyday's preoccupation with metre frequently led him to pay too little regard to the meaning, and his translations are often inept and sometimes bizarre. His Pyrrha is unaccountably prim, with her hair pleated and 'arrayed in homely cloathes', whereas his Chloe (*Carm.*, 1.23) seems more lascivious than the original warrants, when he translates *sequi viro* as 'ripe for Venus' play' (1–12):

> Chloe, thou shunn'st me like wanton Fawn
> Of tim'rous Dam forsook in pathless lawn;
> Dreading with mind agast
>   Ev'ry bush and ev'ry blast.
> For as when Zephyrus trembling leaves doth shake,
> Or green-speckt Newts make Bramble-bushes quake,
> So tremulous is she,
>   Dith'ring both in heart and knee
> But I not to devour thee now pursue,
> As Afric Lyons, and wild Tygers do.
> O leave thy mother pray,
>   Now grown ripe for Venus' play.

Here *montibus* becomes 'lawn', for the sake of a rhyme with 'fawn'. The first line lacks an indefinite article with 'fawn' but adds the gratuitous 'wanton', though the poet's complaint seems to be precisely that Chloe is not wanton enough. The ninth line with its curious word-order needs the Latin to make its meaning plain.

Carm., 11.5 illustrates Holyday at his worst, in serious trouble with Horace's (traditional) comparison of a young girl with a heifer (1–4):

> As yet with neck subdu'd she cannot 'bide
> The yoke, nor answer th' office of a Bride;
> Nor sustain the eagerfull,
>   Fierce rushes of a pondrous Bull.

Already in some confusion as to whether he is describing a girl or a cow, he once again takes Horace's metaphor literally, and implores his reader to 'restrain all longing for Grapes immature' and leaves him with wholly ambiguous (and by now doubtfully relevant) pictures of Chloris, Pholoe and Gyges.

In 1652, the year in which Hawkins's translation was reissued,

Sir Richard Fanshawe published his translation of *Selected Parts of Horace*. Fanshawe (1608–66) is more famous for his translations than for his original compositions; in addition to Horace, he translated Guarini's *Il Pastor Fido*, Camoens' *Lusiad* and Book IV of the *Aeneid*. Fanshawe admired Horace particularly for his philosophy, describing him as 'of all Latin Poets the fullest fraught with Excellent Morality', and he appreciated the Horatian blend of gravity and wit.

Fanshawe's main achievement is in the great variety of metres he uses in his translations; if we do not count Holyday's attempts to reproduce Horace's own metres, Fanshawe is the first to break away from rhymed couplets written in very regular metres. Though not always successful, Fanshawe attempts to convey the particular qualities of Horace's style. He tries at times to catch Horace's terseness (III.7. 13–16):

> She tells how the false woman wrought
> On credulous Pretus, till she brought
> A cruel death upon
> Too chaste Bellerophon.

At his best, Fanshawe creates an English version of the original, not keeping every word or translating literally, but writing idiomatically and sometimes beautifully. Thus he gives 'brooks late swoln with rain' for *decrescentia flumina*, and 'ashes we are and shades' for *pulvis et umbra sumus* (both in *Carm.*, IV.7), and in the same ode (7–13):

> That thou must die, the years and howers say
> Which draw the winged day.
> First Spring, then Summer, that away doth chase,
> And must itself give place
> To Apple-bearing Autumn, and that past,
> Dull winter comes at last.
> But the decays of Time, Time doth repair;

which leaves out half of what Horace wrote and alters the rest slightly, but catches the general sense and spirit of the original.

Where the modern reader finds Fanshawe's translations disappointing is in his habit of embellishing his original by turning Horace's metaphors into elaborate conceits. Compare this part of *Carm.*, I.13 with Ashmore's version, quoted above (6–16):

The warm sap
Wheesing through either Eye,
    Showes with what lingring Flames I frie.
I frie; when thy white hue
    Is in a tavern brawl dy'd blew,
Or when the sharp-set Youth
    Thy melting kiss grinds with his Tooth,
Believ't, his love's not sound
    That can such healing kisses wound;
Kisses which Venus hath
    Made supple in a Nectar bath.

The last volume to be considered is *The Poems of Horace* (1666), a collection of translations selected by Alexander Brome. Brome admired Horace for 'the wit and truth of his excellent sayings' and claims to have read him even when forbidden: 'The same temptation which induced our Grandame Eve to eat fruit, prevaild with me to read Horace, meerly because forbidden.' He puts forward his compilation as 'rude and imperfect draughts', and though this is undoubtedly merely a formal disclaimer, Brome was quite serious in asking his readers for emendations and improvements, and the second edition (in 1671) is substantially changed; amongst other alterations all but one of Holyday's translations are replaced, mainly by those of Thomas Platman. His method of selecting translations for inclusion in the 1666 edition was somewhat haphazard; he began with Fanshawe's translations (which he clearly liked); what Fanshawe had not translated, he supplied from *All Horace his Lyrics*; the remainder came from various friends and acquaintances, and he himself translated twelve satires and eleven epistles.[38] The volume concludes with Jonson's translation of the *Ars Poetica*.

In addition, there are three translations by Abraham Cowley, then at the height of his fame. Cowley's versions are not translations but paraphrases, as he says elsewhere of another translation,[39] 'not exactly copied but rudely imitated'. Cowley, who enjoyed enormous success in his own time, played a large part in establishing the reputation of Horace: he described him as 'the next best Poet in the world to Virgil',[40] but we can guess that Horace really held first, not second, place in his affections. His works are studded with Horatian allusion and quotation, and he

wrote both in poetry and prose on the *Beatus ille* theme, citing the
authority of Horace frequently in his essays when arguing the
advantages of contentment and the simple life. Brome included
Cowley's version of the second part of *Satires* II.6 (the delightful
story of the Town Mouse and the Country Mouse).[41] His
Pindarique odes had their starting place in his admiration for
Horace's imitations of Pindar, and Brome includes Cowley's
version of *Carm.*, IV.2 in the style of a Pindaric ode, very appro-
priately since in this ode Horace himself praises Augustus in
Pindaric style (5 ff.):

> So Pindar does new words and figures roul
> Down his impetuous Dithyrambique tide,
>> Which in no Channel Daignst' abide,
>> Which neither bankes nor dikes controul,
>> Whither th'immortal Gods he sings
>> In a no less immortal strain,
> Or the great acts of God-descended Kings,
> Who in his numbers still survive and raign.
>> Each rich Embroidred line,
>> By his Sacred hand is bound;
> Which their triumphant brows around,
>> Does all their Starrie-Diadems out-shine.

The third Cowley paraphrase is the Pyrrha ode.

The versions of Brome's friends are none of them inspiring,
though they vary in their degree of success. Many have the same
monotonous regularity of rhythm as Hawkins's (*Epodes*, 2. 51 ff.):

> If any such a storm our friend,
> Thundring upon the Seas, does send,
> A turky-cock won't down with me,
> Nor can the Jovian Moorhens be
> More toothsome then the Olive-tree;

with the word-order determined by rhyme and metre rather than
sense (*Carm.*, III.9. 1–4):

> Whilest I alone was dear to thee,
>> And onely chief in thy embrace,
> No Persian King liv'd life to me,
>> Or half so blest or happy was.

Several of the translations embellish Horace with additional metaphors and conceits (as Fanshawe had done). The anonymous paraphrase of *Carm.*, IV.7 translates Horace's *coma* (so frequently used of foliage that it is barely a metaphor) as 'Perucks', adding a touch of unintentional hilarity to the line, and converts the *decrescentia flumina* into 'Each River in Consumption' by adding an equally inappropriate image; this paraphrase in fact succeeds only where it departs from the letter of the original, conveying at least the spirit of the original (but with due debt to Fidele's song) (15 ff.):

> Where wealthy men and worthy too,
> Must all lay down their heads at last
> When their needless toyls are past.

Brome's own translations are all really poor efforts, possibly the weakest in the volume. He conveys Horace's meaning loosely, omitting a great deal. He tries to write in rhymed couplets and in iambic pentameters, but often fails to maintain the metre, especially where the rhyme falls on words of weak stress:

> Or fruitful Asian hills and plains, or what
> The Learned troop of Drusius will be at (*Ep* 1.3. 7–8).

> And leave of pilferring out of Books that be
> By others writ, and plac'd i' th' Library (*Ep* 1.3. 29–30).

> And on the Holy-dayes, when there were no
> Pleadings, to Philips Country-house they go (*Ep* 1.7. 159–60).

He substitutes contemporary figures for the contemporaries of Horace who appear in the *Satires* and *Epistles*, which is entirely in keeping with the spirit of the original, though frustrating to the modern reader who cannot easily identify the people involved!

The century after the first English translation of Horace made its contribution to the understanding of Horace in two ways, in the wealth of translations, versions and paraphrases it produced and by attaching to the *Odes* an importance previously reserved only for the *Satires* and *Epistles*. By the inclusion of Cowley, Brome's volume points us forward to a new era which felt less and less obliged to justify the reading of classical authors on purely moral grounds, and which for many reasons found Horace peculiarly attractive.[42] The *Satires* and *Epistles* had an appeal all of their own in an age which saw a great revival of interest in satire, and the popularity of the ode in the eighteenth century was indirectly due to the influence of Horace. For although it was not Horace whom men strove to imitate but Pindar (with some exceptions, Marvell's *Horatian Ode* being the most notable), it was through Horace's imitations of Pindar that many men first gained their knowledge of the Greek poet.

But one cannot measure the influence of Horace solely in terms of imitations and allusions, for men who loved Horace were attracted by his elegance and precision, his almost Flaubertian exactness in choosing words combined with an ease of expression wholly unlike Flaubert, his ability to mingle light-hearted worldly-wisdom with profound observations on the human condition. In cultivating these qualities in the writings of his admirers, the influence of Horace was incalculably diffuse and immeasurably great.

The earliest English translations of Horace

Date	Translator		Wing or STC number*
1565	Lewis Evans	The Fyrst twoo satars or poyses of Horace	Not available
1566	Thomas Drant	A Medicinable Morall	STC 13805
1567	Thomas Drant	Horace his arte of poetrie, pistles and satyrs Englished	STC 13797
1621	John Ashmore	Certain selected Odes of Horace English by John Ashmore	STC 13799
1627	Sir Thomas Hawkins	Odes and four epodes	STC 13800
		(enlarged edns in 1631, 1635 and 1638)	
1638	Henry Rider	All the Odes and Epodes (2nd edn in 1644)	STC 13804
1640	Ben Jonson	Q. Horatius Flaccus: his Art of Poetry. Englished by Ben Jonson	STC 13798

*Short Title Catalogue of Books Printed in England, Scotland, Ireland, Wales and British America and of English Books Printed in others countries, 1641–1700, compiled by Donald Wing (New York, 1945–51).

Short Title Catalogue of Books Printed in England, Scotland and Ireland, 1475–1640, ed. A. W. Pollard and G. R. Redgrave (London, 1963).

1649	John Smith	*The Lyrick poet, odes and satyres*	Wing H 2772
1652	Sir Thomas Hawkins	*Horace the best of Lyrick poets*	Wing H 2770
1652	Sir Richard Fanshawe	*Selected parts of Horace, Prince of Lyricks*	Wing H 2786
1653	Barton Holyday	*All Horace his lyrics*	Wing H 2776
1666	Various	*The Poems of Horace.* Coll. Alexander Brome (2nd edn 1671)	Wing H 2781

Notes

For a general survey of the reputation of Horace before 1700, see:

MANITIUS, MAX, *Analekten zur Geschichte des Horaz im Mittelalter (bis 1300),* Gottingen, 1893.

STEMPLINGER, EDUARD. *Das Fortleben der Horazischen Lyrik siet der Renaissance,* Leipzig, 1906.

—— *Horaz im Urteil der Jahrhunderte,* Leipzig, 1921.

SHOWERMAN, GRANT, *Horace and his Influence,* London, 1922.

WILKINSON, L. P., *Horace and his Lyric Poetry,* Cambridge, 1945, chapter 7.

BOLGAR, R. R., *The Classical Heritage and its Beneficiaries,* Cambridge, 1954.

1 *Epistola XXII* Ad Eustachium.
2 x.1.96.
3 J. D. A. Ogilvy, *Books Known to the English, 597–1066,* Cambridge, Mass., 1967, pp. 162–3
4 M. L. W. Laistner, 'The Library of the Venerable Bede', in A. H. Thompson, *Bede, His Life, Times and Writings,* Oxford, 1935, p. 242.
5 *Poetae Latini Aevi Carolini,* ed. E. Duemller, L. Traube, K. Strecker and P. de Winterfeld (Monumenta Germaniae Historica: Poetae Latini medii aevi), vol. I, Berlin, 1880, pp. 203–4.
6 *Scholia Vindobonensia ad Horatii artem Poeticam,* ed. Joseph Zechmeister, Vienna, 1887.
7 Max Manitius, *Handschriften antiker Autoren in mittelalterlichen Bibliotheks-Katalogen,* Leipzig, 1935; and see also R. R. Bolgar, *The Classical Heritage and its Beneficiaries,* Cambridge, 1954, p. 413.
8 Gustavus Becker, *Catalogi Bibliothecarum Antiqui,* Bonn, 1885, p. 110.
9 *Dictionnaire d'archéologie chrétienne et de liturgie,* 15 vols, Paris, 1907–53, vol. 2, s.v. 'Fleury'.
10 M. L. W. Laistner, *Thought and Letters in Western Europe* A.D. *500 to 900,* 2nd edn, London, 1957, p. 235, in which Laistner states incorrectly that a copy of Horace is recorded at Bobbio in the late ninth century. In the long and detailed Bobbio catalogue of this date, Horace is conspicuous by his absence. See Becker, op. cit., pp. 64–73.
11 See n. 7 above.

12 M. D. Knowles, 'The Preservation of the Classics', *The English Library before 1700*, ed. F. Wormald and C. E. Wright, London, 1958, p. 145.

13 C. H. Haskins, 'A List of Text-Books from the Close of the Twelfth Century', *Harvard Studies in Classical Philology*, xx (1900), 75 ff.

14 For Conrad of Hirsau see Conrad of Hirschau, *Dialogus super auctores siue Didascalion*, ed. Schwepps, Wurzburg, 1889. Quoted by Bolgar, p. 423. And for both authors see E. R. Curtius, *European Literature and the Latin Middle Ages*, trans. W. R. Trask, London, 1953, pp. 49–50.

15 Quoted by Eduard Stemplinger, *Horaz im Urteil der Iahrhunderte*, Leipzig, 1921, p. 50. For the relative popularity of the different works of Horace from the ninth to the thirteenth century see M. Manitius, *Analekten zur Geschichte des Horaz im Mittelalter (bis 1300)*, Gottingen, 1893, *passim*, and Stemplinger, p. 50.

16 R. A. B. Mynors, 'The Latin Classics known to Boston of Bury', in *Fritz Saxl 1890–1948: A Volume of Memorial Essays from his Friends in England*, ed. D. J. Gordon, Edinburgh, 1957, pp. 199–207.

17 For a good general survey of the English grammar school in the fifteenth and sixteenth centuries, see T. W. Baldwin, *William Shakspere's Small Latine and Lesse Greeke*, Urbana, 1944, vol. i.

18 Quoted by Baldwin, op. cit., p. 103.

19 *Titus Andronicus* IV.ii.19–23.

20 See Baldwin, op. cit., ii, pp. 516 ff.

21 This was the Archdeacon Drant who was quoted as an authority on classical prosody in the correspondence between Spenser and Harvey. See H. S. V. Jones, *A Spenser Handbook*, New York, 1930, pp. 391–3. I owe this information to Mrs E. E. Duncan-Jones.

22 This is presumably only a spelling of 'manners'.

23 The volume contains several epigrams dedicated to Yorkshire worthies, including several to the members of the Fairfax family and 'A speech made to the King's Maiestie comming in his progress to Ripon'; one of the prefatory verses is by Samuel Pullein, a native of Ripley, who graduated from Cambridge, and returned to Ripley as Rector in middle age; the volume is dedicated to the Archbishop of York.

24 Eduard Fraenkel, *Horace*, Oxford, 1957, pp. 184–5.

25 These comprise pagan poems under the heading 'The praise of a Country Life' and Christian ones 'Of a Blessed Life'. In 'The praise of a Country Life' there are translations of Martial's Epigram IV.90, entitled by Ashmore 'De Rusticatione', the last section of Virgil's Second *Georgic*, beginning 'O fortunatos nimium' and Flaminio's 'Umbrae Frigidula'. 'Of a Blessed Life' contains translations of the first Psalm ('Beatus vir', which is itself a prescription for the good life) and poems by Fabricius and Flaminio; it opens with a Martial's Epigram x.47 and a Christian answer by Strigillius, which attacks the whole classical concept of the happy life, sternly exhorting man to remember his sinful state. These poems are all linked in theme to Epode II and *Carm.*, II.16 and 18; they praise the simple life of the countryman, not in the idyllic manner of the pastoral, but emphasizing the actual details of country life. In making this compilation Ashmore earned the distinction of first introducing into England

the vogue for the *Beatus ille* theme which had enormous popularity in the seventeenth century. For a general survey of the *Beatus ille* theme in England see Maren–Sofie Røstvig, *The Happy Man: Studies in the Metamorphoses of a Classical Ideal*, vol. I, *1600–1700*, 2nd edn, Oslo, 1962.

26 Røstvig, op. cit., p. 15.

27 Ibid., p. 16.

28 Ashmore may have been familiar with 'sad cypress' from *The Faerie Queene* or from *Twelfth Night*.

29 'Arrounds' ('encompass', 'flow around') is coined by Hawkins and used also in *Carm.*, 1.7. No other use is listed in *NED*, in which the translation of *Carm.*, 1.31 is incorrectly ascribed to Barton Holyday.

30 The first translation seems to be a curiosity confined to Rider.

31 Readily available in *Ad Pyrrham: A Polyglot Collection of Translations of Horace's Ode to Pyrrha* (1. 5), assembled and with an Introduction by Ronald Storrs, Oxford, 1959, p. 33.

32 Ben Jonson, *Works*, ed. C. H. Herford and Percy Simpson, Oxford, 1925–52, vol. ii, pp. 397–8.

33 Vol. viii, p. 642.

34 Text most readily available in Herford and Simpson, op. cit., vol. viii, pp. 303–37.

35 *reducta*: Jonson is not alone in taking it to mean 'bending'; the anonymous translator whose paraphrase is printed in Brome's collection translates it as 'twisting'.

36 Vol. viii, p. 290.

37 For example in the *DNB*.

38 The contributors are identified by H. F. Brooks, *NQ*, March 1938, 200–1.

39 His translation of *Carm*, III.i, which was not included by Brome.

40 *Of Agriculture.*

41 Note also the version by Wye Saltonstall, *The Country house and the City house or A merry morrall Fable, enlarged out of Horace*. Only the 2nd edn (1637) survives.

42 A detailed study of Horatian allusion and quotation in the eighteenth century has been made by Caroline Goad, *Horace in the English Literature of the Eighteenth Century*, Yale, 1918.

Subject Index

Aceruntia, 34
adjectives, ornamental, 35-7
admonition, 17, 20, 50
adultery, 73, 90
Aeolic poems, 10, 35
Ages of Man, 120, 122, 130-1
Alcaics, 11, 15, 108
Alexandrian poets, 10-12, 21, 23, 117, 121
allegory, 15, 37, 109, 125, 136
alliteration, 119
anatomical juxtaposition, 54-6
Anglo-Saxon authors, 137
antithesis, 29-35, 48-9, 55-6; *see also* contrast
apostrophe, 16
Archilochean iambus, 92
Ars Poetica, 8, 52, 55, 56, 108, 113-34, 137, 138, 141, 148-9, 153
art, 60, 84-92, 108
asclepiads, 10, 15, 146
astrology, 18
Attic tragedy, 16
Augustan poets, 15, 24
autobiography, 98, 100-1

banter, 46-7
Bantia, 35
Beneventum, 67
betrayal, 10-11
Brundisium, 65

caricature, 115, 116, 123, 125-6
Carmen Saeculare, vii, 12, 140, 142-8, 150-2, 154-5, 158
Carolingian era, 137
characterization, 6, 24, 26
Christianity, 135-6
cithara, 26
colours, 37
comedy, 86-7, 118

contrast, 4-5, 35-52, 70, 103; *see also* antithesis
counterpoint, 48-9
criticism, 98, 100-1, 126
Cynics, 78

death, 108-9
demonology, 18
dialogue, 103-4
diction, 44-52, 118-19
discord, 43-4
dissimile, 39
dithyramb, 22
drama, 35-7, 118-23

eclecticism, 99
Eclogues, 9, 59, 136, 139
education, 105, 121, 126, 136, 139
elegy, 10
emulation, 9, 10
encomiastic poetry, 6, 23, 28
epic, 116, 118, 119, 127
Epicureans, 26, 99, 100
epigrams, 10, 37
epistles, 94-7
Epistles, vii, 4, 6, 13, 21, 39, 40, 58, 96-108, 109, 113, 126, 130, 136, 137, 138, 141, 155-6
Epodes, vii, 31, 45, 139, 140, 143, 145, 149, 158
ethics, 72, 96-7, 100, 123, 125
Etruria, 18

Gnatia, 67
Golden Age poetry, 99
Golden Mean, 48-9, 51, 107, 108
golden plectrum, 13
Greek literature, 9, 16, 23, 27, 39, 97, 114, 119, 121, 124
Greek metres, 31
Greek philosophy, 12, 59, 103

161